# Asterisk Gateway Interface 1.4 and 1.6 Programming

Design and develop Asterisk-based VoIP telephony platforms and services using PHP and PHPAGI

**Nir Simionovich**

[PACKT PUBLISHING]

BIRMINGHAM - MUMBAI

# Asterisk Gateway Interface 1.4 and 1.6 Programming

Copyright © 2009 Packt Publishing

All rights reserved. No part of this book may be reproduced, stored in a retrieval system, or transmitted in any form or by any means, without the prior written permission of the publisher, except in the case of brief quotations embedded in critical articles or reviews.

Every effort has been made in the preparation of this book to ensure the accuracy of the information presented. However, the information contained in this book is sold without warranty, either express or implied. Neither the author, Packt Publishing, nor its dealers or distributors will be held liable for any damages caused or alleged to be caused directly or indirectly by this book.

Packt Publishing has endeavored to provide trademark information about all the companies and products mentioned in this book by the appropriate use of capitals. However, Packt Publishing cannot guarantee the accuracy of this information.

First published: January 2009

Production Reference: 1220109

Published by Packt Publishing Ltd.
32 Lincoln Road
Olton
Birmingham, B27 6PA, UK.

ISBN 978-1-847194-46-6

www.packtpub.com

Cover Image by Parag Kadam (paragvkadam@gmail.com)

# Credits

**Author**
Nir Simionovich

**Reviewers**
Brandon Kruse
Suresh Kumar Singampalli
Kimberly Collins

**Acquisition Editor**
Rashmi Phadnis

**Development Editor**
Dhiraj Chandiramani

**Technical Editor**
Gaurav Datar

**Copy Editor**
Sumathi Shridhar

**Editorial Team Leader**
Akshara Aware

**Production Editorial Manager**
Abhijeet Deobhakta

**Project Team Leader**
Lata Basantani

**Project Coordinator**
Lata Basantani

**Indexer**
Monica Ajmera

**Proofreader**
Dirk Manuel

**Production Coordinator**
Rajni R. Thorat

**Cover Work**
Rajni R. Thorat

# About the author

**Nir Simionovich** has been involved with the open source community in Israel since 1997. His involvement started back in 1997, when he was a student at Technion—Israel's Technology Institute—in Haifa. Nir quickly became involved in organizing open source venues and events, promoting the use of Linux and open source technologies in Israel.

In 1998, Nir started working for an IT consulting company (artNET experts Ltd.), where he began to introduce Linux-based solutions for enterprises and banks. By the year 2000, Nir had become a SAIR/GNU certified Linux trainer and administrator, slowly educating the future generations of Linux admins.

In 2001, Nir moved to the cellular content market, working for a mobile content delivery company (m-Wise Inc.—OTC.BB: MWIS.OB). During his commission at m-Wise, Nir successfully migrated a company—built purely on Windows 2000 and ColdFusion—to open source technologies, such as Mandrake Linux (today Mandriva), Apache Tomcat, and Kannel (an open source SMS/WAP gateway).

By 2006, Nir had co-founded Atelis (Atelis PLC—AIM: ATEL). Atelis is a Digium distributor and integrator. During the course of 2006, Nir developed an Asterisk-based international operator services platform for Bezeq International, which replaced a Nortel DMS-300 switch. This platform is currently in use by Bezeq International in Israel, serving over 4000 customer a day.

In mid 2007, Nir left Atelis to become a freelance Asterisk promoter and consultant. Nir is currently providing Asterisk consulting and development services for various companies, ranging from early-stage start-up companies, through VoIP service providers and VoIP equipment vendors. Nir is the founder of the Israeli Asterisk users group. In his spare time, he acts as the website maintainer of the group, and an Asterisk developer, dealing mainly with the localization aspects of Asterisk to Israel.

Coming to 2008, Nir's company (Greenfield Technologies Ltd) won the Digium Innovation award at AstriCon 2008, in the pioneer division—for its implementation of a phone-based prayer system, allowing people from around the world to pray at the western wall in Jerusalem.

# Acknowledgement

I enjoyed writing this book. I hope you will enjoy reading it, and I really look forward to hear from you about your latest Asterisk creation.

I would like to take this opportunity to thank some people:

First of all, I'd like to thank my wife for putting up with my rants and raves about open source—Asterisk, and for putting up with the amount of hardware and mess on my desk, and my complete disregard to anything in the house. Nili, I love you.

To my parents, for putting up with my craziness over the years and the endless nights of me tapping at the console when I was growing up.

To Mark Spencer, thank you for developing Asterisk™ and for creating one of the most innovative tools on the market today. And most importantly, thank you for your help back in 2003, when I needed to install the first BRI interface, and I had no idea what I was doing in there—Mark was back then sitting in the IRC channel, and was one of the biggest helps to me.

To Schuyler Deerman, who actually connected me with Packt for the publishing of my previous book, which has also led to the writing of this book. Schuyler is one of Digium's field marketing people and has become a close and personal friend over the course of our mutual work. Schuyler is currently located in Berlin, Germany.

To Optimus, my first Asterisk™ server, which suffered and suffered and suffered, untill I got it to work as I wanted it. Optimus is currently resting in pieces, somewhere down the pile of servers I have at home.

# About the reviewers

**Suresh Kumar Singampalli** has more than four years of experience in various languages (C/C++, Java and .Net) and technologies for IVR and VOIP (Asterisk, OCS) platforms. Apart from developing products for IVR platforms, he has been doing research on various open source and Microsoft-related VOIP platforms. He works for LeadingC Pvt Ltd., and right now he is doing his research on TextToSpeech and Speech Recognition technologies for embedded and desktop applications.

> I would like to thank my brother Sanjeet and my friends—Anantgiri, Mohan, Srinivas, and Pavan, who have helped me in reviewing this book.

**Brandon Kruse** loves and lives Asterisk. Asterisk has enabled the world to become a better place. Digium is the company that sponsors and produces this software that is revolutionizing the long-commercialized telephony industry.

> I would like to say thanks to my family—particularly my dad, Eric Kruse—for molding my mind as a young boy, to find a need and fill it, to think outside the box, and for the numerous amount of advice that I could never pay him back for, and that got me where I am today. And finally, a bigger thanks for pushing me to never give up on my dreams. "Thanks to my mom, for always being there for me".
>
> I would also like to give a token of thanks to Mark Spencer, for giving me this incredible opportunity, for being a pioneer in a dark industry, for being my mentor, friend, and an amazing entrepreneur.
>
> Finally I would thank Lauren, my girlfriend, for always putting up with me, and my engineer type nature during this process. It takes a lot to love a geek, especially when Asterisk takes time away from us, and yet she sticks through it, and even debugs my code!

**Kimberly Collins** is a California transplant who found her home in Austin, TX. She has worked in the field of Information Technology and communications for over ten years. She has spent the last two years working for one of the largest hosting companies in the world, and is currently one of the lead administrators and developers of their global VOIP infrastructure.

# Table of Contents

**Preface**   1
**Chapter 1: Installing a 'Vanilla' Asterisk**   7
  **Downloading Asterisk**   8
  **Zaptel—Zapata Telephony Driver**   9
  **DAHDI—Digium Asterisk Hardware Device Interface**   10
  **Libpri—ISDN PRI Library**   10
  **Asterisk—the open source PBX**   11
  **Asterisk-addons—the open source PBX**   11
  **Asterisk—SVN source packages**   12
    Obtaining the source code packages from SVN   12
    Compilation dependencies   13
  **Compiling the source code**   13
    Compiling and installing Zaptel   14
      Step 1: Configure   14
      Step 2: Define the options you would like to compile   15
      Step 3: Compiling and installing   16
    Compiling and installing DAHDI   18
      Step 1: Compile the kernel module   18
      Step 2: Install the dahdi kernel module   18
      Step 3: Compile the dahdi-tools package   20
      Step 4: Configure the dahdi-tools to be installed   20
      Step 5: Compile and install dahdi-tools   21
    Differences between Zaptel and DAHDI   21
    Compiling and installing libpri   22
    Compiling and installing Asterisk   23
      Step 1: Configure   23
      Step 2: Define the options you would like to compile   23
      Step 3: Compiling the code   26
  **Summary**   29

## Chapter 2: Basic IVR Development: Using the Asterisk DialPlan — 31
### The dialplan is a set of "finite state machines" — 32
### The dialplan syntax — 33
#### The extension — 33
##### Inclusion of contexts — 34
##### The [general] and [global] contexts — 35
##### Extension pattern matching — 35
##### Special extensions — 36
#### Dialplan Switches — 37
#### Variables, applications, and functions — 37
##### Variables—built-in and custom — 37
#### Applications and functions — 41
##### Your first IVR application — 41
### Summary — 53

## Chapter 3: More IVR Development: Input, Recordings, and Call Control — 55
### Grabbing and processing user input — 55
#### The Read application — 56
#### Branching—Goto, GotoIf, Gosub, and GosubIf — 58
##### Goto and GotoIf — 59
##### Writing expressions — 61
##### Regular expressions — 62
##### Gosub and GosubIf — 63
##### Exec, ExecIf, and TryExec — 65
#### Macros—Macro and MacroExclusive — 67
##### Additional Asterisk applications — 69
#### Self exploration — 73
### Summary — 73

## Chapter 4: A Primer to AGI: Asterisk Gateway Interface — 75
### How does AGI work? — 75
#### EAGI, DeadAGI and FastAGI — 77
##### EAGI—Enhanced Asterisk Gateway Interface — 77
##### DeadAGI—execution on hangup — 77
##### FastAGI—AGI execution via a TCP socket — 78
##### AGI scripting frameworks — 80
#### The AGI application — 80
#### The AGI execution flow — 81
#### The AGI methods API — 83
### The ten rules of AGI development — 84
#### Rule #1: An AGI script should terminate as fast as possible — 85
#### Rule #2: Blocking applications have no place in AGI — 85
#### Rule #3: Asterisk channels are stateful—use them — 85
#### Rule #4: AGI scripts should manipulate data—no more — 86

| | |
|---|---|
| Rule #5: VM based languages are bad for AGI scripting | 86 |
| Rule #6: Binary-compiled AGI is not always the answer | 86 |
| Rule #7: Balance your scripts with dialplan logic | 87 |
| Rule #8: Balance your scripts with web services | 87 |
| Rule #9: Syslog is your friend—use it | 88 |
| Rule #10: The Internet is for Asterisk | 88 |
| **A preface to what's coming ahead** | **89** |
| **Summary** | **90** |

## Chapter 5: AGI Scripting with PHP — 91

| | |
|---|---|
| **PHP-CLI vs. PHP-CGI** | **91** |
| **The php.ini configuration file** | **92** |
| **AGI script permissions** | **92** |
| **The structure of a PHP based AGI script** | **93** |
| **Communication between Asterisk and AGI** | **94** |
| **The AGI Hello-World program** | **95** |
| **AGI debugging** | **100** |
| **Summary** | **101** |

## Chapter 6: PHPAGI: An AGI Class Library in PHP — 103

| | |
|---|---|
| **Obtaining PHPAGI** | **104** |
| **The file structure of PHPAGI** | **104** |
| **A very simple PHPAGI example** | **104** |
| **The AGI/Dialplan high-wire act** | **106** |
| Introducing Atomic-AGI | 107 |
| Atomic-AGI—a dialplan example | 108 |
| SetSessionID.agi—meet your state maintainer | 108 |
| agiWrapper.agi—an all purpose AGI execution wrapper | 110 |
| **A slightly more complex PHPAGI example** | **114** |
| db_validate_target.inc.php | 117 |
| db_register_cdr.inc.php | 119 |
| **AGI Scripts in popular Asterisk applications** | **119** |
| FreePBX™—the most popular Asterisk management GUI | 119 |
| A2Billing™—a pre-paid calling card system | 120 |
| **Summary** | **121** |

## Chapter 7: FastAGI: AGI as a TCP Server — 123

| | |
|---|---|
| **FastAGI argument handling** | **124** |
| Asterisk 1.2.X and 1.4.X | 125 |
| Asterisk 1.6.X | 125 |
| **FastAGI error handling** | **125** |
| Asterisk 1.2.X | 126 |
| Asterisk 1.4.X and 1.6.X | 126 |

## FastAGI with PHPAGI and xinetd — 126
- Introducing xintetd—the Internet services daemon — 127
- Configuring xinetd for FastAGI and PHPAGI — 127
- Configuring PHPAGI for FastAGI — 130
- The fastagiWrapper.php bootstrap — 130
- Performance consideration — 133

## FastAGI with PHPAGI and Google — 133
## FastAGI with other tool kits — 140
- Asterisk::FastAGI—a PERL module for FastAGI handling — 140
- Asterisk-JAVA—a Java package for Asterisk — 141

## Summary — 142

# Chapter 8: AMI: The Asterisk Manager Interface — 143
## AMI—the history — 143
- How does AMI work? — 144
- AMI with Asterisk 1.0 and 1.2 — 145
- AMI with Asterisk 1.4 and 1.6 — 146

## AMI–understanding basics — 146
- Events and Actions — 146
- Logging in to the Manager Interface — 147
- Sending actions to the Manager Interface — 147
- Logging off from the Manager Interface — 148

## PHPAGI and the AMI Interface — 148
- Direct AMI interface invocation — 148
- AMI interface invocation via the PHPAGI class — 149
- Interacting with the AMI interface — 150
  - Sending actions to the AMI inteface — 150
  - Event callbacks from AMI interface — 151
- PHPAGI AMI originate quirk — 152

## Click-2-Call and Web-Callback — 155
- Demystifying the Asterisk Originate manager action — 155
- Welcome to Jabka—the world's favourite Click-2-Call — 156
- AMI proxy servers — 158
- AJAM—AJAX Enabled Manager — 158

## Summary — 159

# Chapter 9: Final Programming Project — 161
## ACRG—Asterisk Call Recording Gateway — 162
- Requirements — 162
- Network connectivity—PSTN — 163

## Project implementation guide — 163
- Step 1: Analysis of the requirements — 164

| | |
|---|---|
| Step 2: Understanding operational constraints | 165 |
| Step 3: Detailed call flow charts | 169 |
| Step 4: The Asterisk dialplan context | 170 |
| Step 5: Develop your human interfaces | 170 |
| Step 6: Test, test, and test again | 171 |
| **Additional programming projects** | **171** |
| Click-2-Call | 171 |
| Jajah.Com | 172 |
| Stateful call masking | 172 |
| Punk'ed call | 174 |
| Date rescue call | 174 |
| Conference bridge | 174 |
| **Summary** | **175** |
| **Chapter 10: Scaling Asterisk Applications** | **177** |
| **Scaling Asterisk platforms** | **178** |
| Database query caching | 179 |
| Starting up | 179 |
| Using it in a script | 180 |
| Utilization of web services | 182 |
| Introduction to XML-RPC | 182 |
| Apache versus Lighttpd | 185 |
| Virtualization and cloud computing | 189 |
| **Summary** | **191** |
| **Index** | **193** |

# Preface

This is my second book, and I have to admit that I really enjoyed working on this book. While I enjoyed working on my previous book, (the *AsteriskNow* book from Packt Publishing), I couldn't help but feel that a portion of me has really slipped into the pages of this book.

This book is a developer's book, and it is written for developers by a developer. I see myself as an Asterisk application developer. After developing dozens of platforms over the course of the past six years, all based arround Asterisk, I can honestly say that I've seen mistakes that I made six years ago, still being made today by novice developers.

My role at Greenfield Technologies Ltd. (apart from being the CEO and Founder) is that of a development consultant, where I render various Asterisk consulting services to various companies in Israel and worldwide. Wherever I go, no matter what customer I cater, the mistakes and wrongful paradigms seem to persist. They persist due to a simple reason: there is no school for Asterisk developers. We have web developers, core developers, and database developers. But Asterisk developer is usually either a web developer or a core developer who is assigned a task, or in the worst case, a database developer entrusted with a task that he totally doesn't understand. The developers automatically do what they were taught to do: they superimpose their aggregated knowledge and experience on the Asterisk world, which usually ends up in disaster.

Asterisk is one of the most innovative pieces of open source software created in the past ten years (Asterisk just hit nine years old on December 05, 2008). While Asterisk provides one of the most extensive telephony toolkits available today, its utilization in a commercial application or platform construct isn't as straightforward as it would seem. This book de-mystifies some of the mystic characteristics associated with Asterisk, while at the same exposing some of the well-guarded secrets of professional Asterisk platform developers.

Asterisk requires a new skill set to be developed—one that web developers have no idea of and core developers completely disregard. My aim with this book is to enable you to learn the lessons and values that I've learned over a period of six years from a simple, shrink wrapped, to the point guide. I hope this book will remain on your table as a useful tool.

# What this book covers

*Chapter 1* introduces the various hardware elements required for installing your Asterisk PBX system, and guides you through the Asterisk installation procedure.

*Chapter* 2 introduces us to the dialplan—extension, context, and syntax. It then covers the main part—developing a basic **IVR (Interactive Voice Response)** application using Asterisk dialplan.

*Chapter 3* takes us a bit deeper into IVR development, wherein we learn grabbing and processing input. The introduction of the Read application, and the conditional branching and execution, enable a new flexibility that was not available initially.

*Chapter 4* is all about AGI—its working, its three types, and the different frameworks. Finally it covers the do's and don'ts that need to be followed for the AGI script to work and function properly.

*Chapter 5* introduces you to your first AGI script, using the `Hello World` program. It also touches upon AGI debugging.

*Chapter 6* covers a PHP based AGI class library—PHPAGI. The chapter starts with an explanation of the PHPAGI file structure, and then goes on to cover simple, and finally more complex, PHPAGI examples.

*Chapter 7* introduces the basic elements of a FastAGI server, again using PHP and PHPAGI.

*Chapter 8* helps understand the **Asterisk Manager Interface (AMI)**—an Asterisk proprietary **Computer Telephony Integration (CTI)** interface.

*Chapter 9* takes you through the steps of developing a full click-2-call application, using all the concepts you've learned. Chapter 9 can be used as the basis for a large scale service, such as JaJah or RebTel.

*Chapter 10* tries to deal with some of the more advanced topics of developing Asterisk applications—mainly scalability and performance issues. By the end of this chapter, the reader should be well-equipped with the information to build the next Verizon Killer application.

> Documentation for Asterisk applications are taken directly from the Asterisk source code and/or command line interface. Documentation for PHPAGI is taken from the PHPAGI website.

## What you need for this book

In order to utilize this book to the fullest, you will need the following:

- A **personal computer** (**PC**) running the Linux operating system. We used CentOS for this book, but you may use any distribution that you feel comfortable with. If you would like to get up and running really quickly, you can use the AsteriskNOW (version 1.5) distribution, located at http://www.asterisknow.org. This can also be a **Virtual Machine** (**VM**) based system, using VMWARE.
- A PC that you can use as your workstation for development purposes and web browsing purposes.
- An IP Phone—either a soft phone or hardware IP phone.
- A Digium TDM11B card (optional). The Digium TDM11B card provides two analog interfaces—one for a phone line (an FXO) and the other for an analog phone (an FXS).
- Experience with the Linux shell—basic system administration skills are required.
- Experience with a programming language. This book is for developers, it doesn't teach you a programming language. Knowledge of PHP is preferred for this book.
- Finally, you need patience and a pot of coffee—at least for the first three chapters.

## Who is this book for

This book is intended for developers wishing to utilize Asterisk, system administrators wishing to gain better control over their Asterisk installation, and telephony service providers wishing to deploy Asterisk-based solutions to their infrastructure. You are expected to have some experience with Asterisk and a basic understanding of programming. No knowledge of Asterisk programming is required.

## Conventions

In this book, you will find a number of styles of text that distinguish between different kinds of information. Here are some examples of these styles, and an explanation of their meaning.

Code words in text are shown as follows: "If we are going to examine the operational flow of the just seen context, it is fairly clear that Asterisk will perform background playback on two files—`demo-congrats` and `demo-instruct`"

A block of code will be set as follows:

```
exten => 3,1,Set(LANGUAGE()=fr)
exten => 3,n,Goto(s,restart)
```

Any command-line input and output is written as follows:

```
# ./memcached -d -m 2048 -l 192.168.2.52 -p 6636
```

**New terms** and **important words** are introduced in a bold-type font. Words that you see on the screen, in menus or dialog boxes for example, appear in our text like this: "As the immediately preceding screenshot illustrates, issue the **make config** command in order to install initial configuration files and system init scripts."

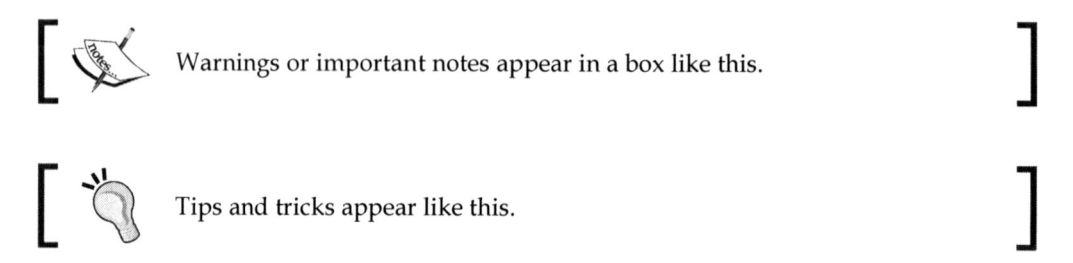

> Warnings or important notes appear in a box like this.

> Tips and tricks appear like this.

## Reader feedback

Feedback from our readers is always welcome. Let us know what you think about this book, what you liked or may have disliked. Reader feedback is important for us to develop titles that you really get the most out of.

To send us general feedback, simply drop an email to feedback@packtpub.com, making sure to mention the book title in the subject of your message.

If there is a book that you need and would like to see us publish, please send us a note in the **SUGGEST A TITLE** form on www.packtpub.com or email suggest@packtpub.com.

If there is a topic that you have expertise in and you are interested in either writing or contributing to a book, see our author guide on www.packtpub.com/authors.

# Customer support

Now that you are the proud owner of a Packt book, we have a number of things to help you to get the most from your purchase.

## Downloading the example code for the book

Visit http://www.packtpub.com/files/code/4466_Code.zip to directly download the example code.

The downloadable files contain instructions on how to use them.

## Errata

Although we have taken every care to ensure the accuracy of our contents, mistakes do happen. If you find a mistake in one of our books — maybe a mistake in text or code — we would be grateful if you would report this to us. By doing this you can save other readers from frustration, and help to improve subsequent versions of this book. If you find any errata, report them by visiting http://www.packtpub.com/support, selecting your book, clicking on the **let us know** link, and entering the details of your errata. Once your errata are verified, your submission will be accepted and the errata are added to the list of existing errata. The existing errata can be viewed by selecting your title from http://www.packtpub.com/support.

## Piracy

Piracy of copyright material on the Internet is an ongoing problem across all media. At Packt, we take the protection of our copyright and licenses very seriously. If you come across any illegal copies of our works in any form on the Internet, please provide the location address or website name immediately so we can pursue a remedy.

Please contact us at `copyright@packtpub.com` with a link to the suspected pirated material.

We appreciate your help in protecting our authors, and our ability to bring you valuable content.

## Questions

You can contact us at `questions@packtpub.com` if you are having a problem with some aspect of the book, and we will do our best to address it.

# 1
# Installing a 'Vanilla' Asterisk

*In order to change the world, you have to get your head together first.*
-Jimi Hendrix

When Mark Spencer initially created Asterisk, he didn't realize the disruptive nature of his code. Just as Jimi Hendrix had a good idea of how he wanted to change the world, so does Mark on where Asterisk is destined to go. Getting our heads together with Asterisk may seem simple, but is more complex than you would imagine. You are probably saying to yourself right now: "Hey I'm a developer with years of experience; I have my head straight and on the money! Let's get coding!" Well, I have some news for you—NO YOU CAN'T!

Over the past five years, as the popularity of Asterisk grew and its install base multiplied at a geometric rate, it suffered an almost identical fate to that of PHP and other open source projects. Asterisk granted the integrators and developers the ability to shape and mould it to suit their needs. However, as Asterisk is an open source project, there was no clear methodology to do so. Thus many people developed a multitude of applications for Asterisk—some turned into huge projects (FreePBX, A2Billing, TrixBox) while others faded away. What made a good project unique? Was it its feature set? Was it a special function that everyone needed? If we examine the early stages of FreePBX (the early versions of FreePBX were called **AMP (Asterisk Management Portal)** and its current version, you wouldn't believe that they were programmed by the same people. This is because the people who invested their time into the project learned from their mistakes and created better applications. Developers and integrators dealing with Asterisk for the first time are usually fully capable of developing applications that work—at least to some extent. By superimposing their traditional development techniques to the Asterisk world, they usually end up developing an application that would work to an extent, but would fail miserably when dealing with the rapidly expanding **IVR (Interactive Voice Response)** services.

*Installing a 'Vanilla' Asterisk*

So how do we get our heads together? Simple! Start from the most basic thing, that is, installing Asterisk from its source code.

> At this point, we would assume that you already have a Linux-based desktop or server for you to use during this book. You can also use a virtual machine for this book. All of the examples and screenshots in this book are taken from a server running on a virtual machine, using VMWare.

## Downloading Asterisk

The best place to obtain the Asterisk source code would be from the Asterisk community website. Point your browser to http://www.asterisk.org, and you should see the screen shown in the following screenshot, from which you can download the code.

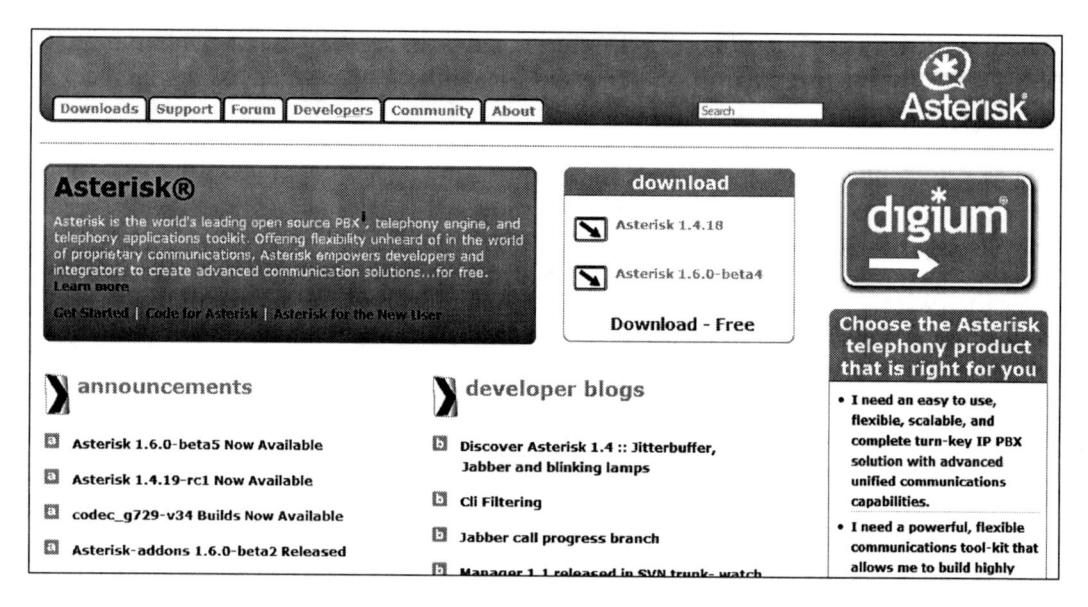

Asterisk is available for download in two distinct versions—a stable release and an SVN release. Apart from Asterisk, there are three additional software packages that you may require for your application to work completely. We shall now explain the usage of the stable software packages, and how to download and compile them. Later on, we shall learn how to download the latest SVN package.

# Zaptel—Zapata Telephony Driver

Let's turn our attention to Zaptel.

> If you intend to use Asterisk version 1.6.X, please skip this section and go to the next.

The Asterisk website describes Zaptel as:

> *Kernel interface device drivers for Analog and Digital interface cards. Digium hardware requires Zaptel drivers.*

In general, Zaptel provides all of the drivers and kernel modules, required to use Asterisk with a TDM connection. The stock kernel drivers available in the Asterisk distribution are compatible with all Digium hardware and Astribank hardware available from Xorcom. In addition to the kernel support for Digium hardware, the Zaptel module also provides a virtual timer kernel module, which is used by Asterisk for allowing conference calls to be made without the physical timer that is provided by Digium hardware.

> Currently, there are various companies manufacturing Zaptel-compatible hardware. However, these hardware devices usually require a patch to the code, or they use an additional software package. Our book will not deal with these.
>
> In general, it is my personal belief that when using an open source product, it is imperative to support the company funding the development—Digium in this case.

The stable Zaptel source code is available as a `tar.gz` file, from the Digium download site. Zaptel stable source code can be downloaded from http://downloads.digium.com/pub/zaptel/. The current stable release would usually be available with the keyword "current", indicating that this is the current stable release.

> At the time of writing this book, the current Zaptel stable release was 1.4.9.2. It is quite likely that by the time this book is published, the Zaptel stable release will be different.

Download the Zaptel source package to your designated Asterisk server, and continue to the next section.

# DAHDI—Digium Asterisk Hardware Device Interface

In version 1.6 of Asterisk, Zaptel has been replaced by the DAHDI framework. Unlike Zaptel, which was both a self-enclosed kernel module and a set of tools, the DAHDI framework has separated these into two distinct packages—dahdi-linux and dahdi-tools.

> You are probably wondering: "What was wrong with the name Zaptel? Couldn't they just create zaptel-linux and zaptel-tools packages?" Well, the reason for the name change was due to a copyright infringement issue where a calling card company called Zaptel had indicated that the name Zaptel was their trademark, long before Asterisk used it—hence the name change.

The stable DAHDI source code is available as a `tar.gz` file, from the Digium download site. The dahdi-linux package can be downloaded from http://downloads.digium.com/pub/telephony/dahdi-linux/ and while dahdi-tools package can be downloaded from http://downloads.digium.com/pub/telephony/dahdi-tools/.

If you are using Asterisk 1.6 as the base of your installation, download the dahdi-linux and dahdi-tools packages, and continue to the next section.

# Libpri—ISDN PRI Library

The Asterisk website describes Libpri as:

> *Primary Rate ISDN (PRI) library for T1/E1/J1 interfaces.*

In general, libpri provides Asterisk a programmatic API, allowing it to interface with ISDN-type interfaces. If you are not using hardware interfaces with your Asterisk installation, or you are not using an ISDN PRI interface, you don't have to install this library.

The stable libpri source code is available as a `tar.gz` file, from the Digium download site. Libpri stable source code can be downloaded from http://downloads.digium.com/pub/libpri/. The current stable release would usually be available with the keyword "current", indicating that this is the current stable release.

> At the time of writing this book, the current libpri stable release is 1.4.3. It is quite likely that by the time this book is published, the libpri stable release will be different, or may come in a completely new major version (1.6.X).

Download the libpri source package to your designated Asterisk server, and continue to the next section.

## Asterisk—the open source PBX

Asterisk doesn't require any introduction. Its source-stable source code is available for download from the Digium website. The source code can be downloaded from http://downloads.digium.com/pub/asterisk/. The current stable release would usually be available with the keyword "current", indicating that this is the current stable release.

> At the time of writing, the current Asterisk stable release was 1.4.22. It is quite likely that by the time this book is published, the Asterisk stable release will be different, or may come in a completely new major version (1.6.X).

Download the Asterisk source package to your designated Asterisk server, and continue to the next section.

## Asterisk-addons—the open source PBX

While Asterisk provides a complete PBX system, some of the modules that people have become used to working with are required to be distributed using an external source package. These usually include packages that require a different licensing scheme, or packages that use other packages for which the licensing scheme doesn't comply with Asterisk's dual licensing scheme.

The Asterisk-addons stable source code is available for download from the Digium website. The source code can be downloaded from http://downloads.digium.com/pub/asterisk/. The current stable release would usually be available with the keyword "current", indicating that this is the current stable release.

*Installing a 'Vanilla' Asterisk*

> At the time of writing, the current Asterisk-addons stable release was 1.4.6. It is quite likely that by the time this book is published, a different stable release version or a completely new major version (1.6.X) may be released.

Download the Asterisk-addons source package to your designated Asterisk server. At this point, you may read the next section dealing with the aspects of using Asterisk SVN version, or continue to the following section dealing with code compilation.

## Asterisk—SVN source packages

Like most software products, Asterisk has had a multitude of versions since its early days. When a group of people are required to work together on the same code base, it is very common to use a code-versioning system that makes sure that while one person works on a certain piece of code, he/she does not overwrite another person's work. In the open source world, there are two main variants to code-versioning systems—CVS and SVN. **CVS** stands for **Concurrent Versions System**, which does exactly what it says. In the early days of the Asterisk project, CVS was used as the code-versioning system. During the course of 2005, Digium shifted from using CVS to using SVN. **SVN** stands for **Subversion**, which is a different method of managing multiple versions of the same source code.

> Code versioning systems are not covered by this book. However, we suggest that if you deal with multiple programmers working on the same source code, do look into using one of these.

## Obtaining the source code packages from SVN

Obtaining the source code packages via SVN is performed by using the SVN utility directly from your Linux command line. In order to do so, first log in to your Linux server as root, and create a directory that would hold your source code packages.

In order to get the source code packages, you are required to use the following commands:

```
# mkdir asterisk-sources
# cd asterisk-sources
# svn checkout http://svn.digium.com/svn/asterisk/trunk asterisk
# svn checkout http://svn.digium.com/svn/dahdi/linux/trunk dahdi-linux
```

```
# svn checkout http://svn.digium.com/svn/dahdi/tools/trunk dahdi-tools
# svn checkout http://svn.digium.com/svn/libpri/trunk libpri
```

> For the rest of this book, we shall restrict ourselves to working on the SVN version of source code.

## Compilation dependencies

In order to compile the various source code packages, some dependencies must be met. In accordance to your Linux distribution, you must install the following packages:

- `gcc`
- `newt-devel`
- `libusb-devel`
- `kernel-devel` (or `kernel-smp-devel` depending on your kernel)
- `glibc-devel`
- `ncurses-devel`
- `openssl-devel`
- `zlib-devel`

These package names are based upon the RedHat/Fedora distribution, so the names on your particular distribution may vary. Using your distribution package manager, install these packages prior to beginning any compilation.

## Compiling the source code

The compilation of the Asterisk project source code is performed in a certain order. The following compilation order must be met, in order for your compiled code to run for the first time.

1. Compile and install the Zaptel kernel module (or the dahdi kernel module).
2. Compile and install the libpri library (applies only if you use ISDN PRI interface cards).
3. Compile and install the Asterisk software.
4. Compile and install the Asterisk-addons module.

*Installing a 'Vanilla' Asterisk*

# Compiling and installing Zaptel

Let's turn our attention to compiling and installing Zaptel.

> If you intend to use Asterisk version 1.6.X or SVN trunk (as we've mentioned before), please skip this section and go to the next one.

Follow the steps mentioned here to compile and install the Zaptel kernel module:

## Step 1: Configure

From within the Zaptel kernel module directory, issue the **./configure** command, to have the compilation script scan your system and configure the proper compilation order.

```
[root@tvms zaptel]# ./configure
checking for gcc... gcc
checking for C compiler default output file name... a.out
checking whether the C compiler works... yes
checking whether we are cross compiling... no
checking for suffix of executables...
checking for suffix of object files... o
checking whether we are using the GNU C compiler... yes
checking whether gcc accepts -g... yes
checking for gcc option to accept ISO C89... none needed
checking how to run the C preprocessor... gcc -E
checking for a BSD-compatible install... /usr/bin/install -c
checking whether ln -s works... yes
checking for GNU make... make
checking for grep... /bin/grep
checking for sh... /bin/sh
checking for ln... /bin/ln
checking for chkconfig... /sbin/chkconfig
checking for wget... /usr/bin/wget
checking for grep that handles long lines and -e... (cached) /bin/grep
checking for egrep... /bin/grep -E
checking for ANSI C header files...
```

## Step 2: Define the options you would like to compile

Zaptel enables the installer to choose which Zaptel modules to include in the compilation order. The selection of modules is performed by issuing the command `make menuconfig` from the command line, and then using the available GUI.

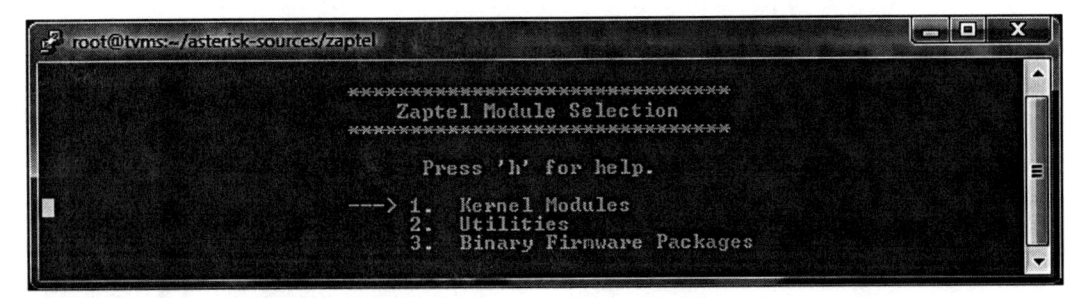

```
*****************************
     Zaptel Module Selection
*****************************
        Press 'h' for help.

---> 1. Kernel Modules
     2. Utilities
     3. Binary Firmware Packages
```

From this menu, you will be able to select which of the kernel modules to compile, and which Zaptel utilities you would like to install. If you are unsure about the modules that you would like to enable or disable, simply press the $q$ key to quit and leave the default settings.

> Zaptel provides a total of eighteen different kernel modules—each one for different hardware. It is possible that by the time you read this book, additional modules will be available, so listing each one of them at this point will be redundant. Consult the Zaptel documentation and the Digium forums for information about each of the kernel modules. Another good source of configuration examples for Zaptel would be the voip-info.org website, at: `http://www.voip-info.org/wiki/view/Asterisk+Data+Configuration`.

*Installing a 'Vanilla' Asterisk*

## Step 3: Compiling and installing

Once you have selected your desired zaptel kernel module configuration, proceed to the actual compilation. The compilation is performed by issuing the command `make all` from the command line, followed by `make install` in order to install the kernel modules, which is then followed by `make config` to install a set of preliminary configuration files.

```
[root@tvms zaptel]# make
make[1]: Entering directory `/root/asterisk-sources/zaptel'
make -C /lib/modules/2.6.18-53.1.14.el5/build SUBDIRS=/root/asterisk-sources/zap
tel/kernel HOTPLUG_FIRMWARE=no KBUILD_OBJ_M="zaptel.o ztd-eth.o ztd-loc.o ztdumm
y.o ztdynamic.o " modules
make[2]: Entering directory `/usr/src/kernels/2.6.18-53.1.14.el5-i686'
  CC [M]  /root/asterisk-sources/zaptel/kernel/zaptel-base.o
  LD [M]  /root/asterisk-sources/zaptel/kernel/zaptel.o
  CC [M]  /root/asterisk-sources/zaptel/kernel/ztd-eth.o
  CC [M]  /root/asterisk-sources/zaptel/kernel/ztd-loc.o
  CC [M]  /root/asterisk-sources/zaptel/kernel/ztdummy.o
  CC [M]  /root/asterisk-sources/zaptel/kernel/ztdynamic.o
  Building modules, stage 2.
  MODPOST
  CC      /root/asterisk-sources/zaptel/kernel/zaptel.mod.o
  LD [M]  /root/asterisk-sources/zaptel/kernel/zaptel.ko
  CC      /root/asterisk-sources/zaptel/kernel/ztd-eth.mod.o
  LD [M]  /root/asterisk-sources/zaptel/kernel/ztd-eth.ko
  CC      /root/asterisk-sources/zaptel/kernel/ztd-loc.mod.o
  LD [M]  /root/asterisk-sources/zaptel/kernel/ztd-loc.ko
  CC      /root/asterisk-sources/zaptel/kernel/ztdummy.mod.o
  LD [M]  /root/asterisk-sources/zaptel/kernel/ztdummy.ko
  CC      /root/asterisk-sources/zaptel/kernel/ztdynamic.mod.o
```

The preceding image shows the actual compilation of the Zaptel kernel module. Once the compilation is completed without errors, issue the `make install` command to install your kernel modules.

```
.8 /usr/share/man/man8/
/usr/bin/install -c -D -m 644 zaptel.conf.sample /etc/zaptel.conf
/usr/bin/install -c -D -m 755 libtonezone.a /usr/lib/libtonezone.a
/usr/bin/install -c -D -m 755 libtonezone.so /usr/lib/libtonezone.so.1.0
if [ `id -u` = 0 ]; then \
                /sbin/ldconfig || : ;\
        fi
rm -f /usr/liblibtonezone.so
/bin/ln -sf libtonezone.so.1.0 \
                /usr/lib/libtonezone.so.1
/bin/ln -sf libtonezone.so.1.0 \
                /usr/lib/libtonezone.so
/sbin/restorecon -v /usr/lib/libtonezone.so
/usr/bin/install -c -D -m 644 tonezone.h /usr/include/zaptel/tonezone.h
/usr/bin/install -c -D -m 644 kernel/zaptel.h /usr/include/zaptel/zaptel.h
###################################################
###
### Zaptel installed successfully.
### If you have not done so before, install init scripts with:
###
###     make config
###
###################################################
[root@tvms zaptel]#
```

As the immediately preceding screenshot illustrates, issue the **make config** command in order to install the initial configuration files and system init scripts.

```
root@tvms:~/asterisk-sources/zaptel
/sbin/restorecon -v /usr/lib/libtonezone.so
/usr/bin/install -c -D -m 644 tonezone.h /usr/include/zaptel/tonezone.h
/usr/bin/install -c -D -m 644 kernel/zaptel.h /usr/include/zaptel/zaptel.h
###############################################################
###
### Zaptel installed successfully.
### If you have not done so before, install init scripts with:
###
###    make config
###
###############################################################
[root@tvms zaptel]# make config
install -D zaptel.init /etc/rc.d/init.d/zaptel
/usr/bin/install -c -D -m 644 zaptel.sysconfig /etc/sysconfig/zaptel
install -D ifup-hdlc /etc/sysconfig/network-scripts/ifup-hdlc
/sbin/chkconfig --add zaptel
Zaptel has been configured.

If you have any zaptel hardware it is now recommended to
edit /etc/default/zaptel or /etc/sysconfig/zaptel and set there an
optimal value for the variable MODULES .

I think that the zaptel hardware you have on your system is:
[root@tvms zaptel]#
```

In order to verify your installation, you may use the **modinfo zaptel** command, which will report information back on your installed kernel module. If the module information is reported back correctly, issue the **service zaptel start** command in order to start the kernel modules.

```
root@tvms:~/asterisk-sources/zaptel
[root@tvms zaptel]# modinfo zaptel
filename:       /lib/modules/2.6.18-53.1.14.el5/misc/zaptel.ko
version:        SVN-branch-1.4-r3979
license:        GPL
description:    Zapata Telephony Interface
author:         Mark Spencer <markster@digium.com>
srcversion:     7EA994ED0AEAFC764C7EB55
depends:        crc-ccitt
vermagic:       2.6.18-53.1.14.el5 SMP mod_unload 686 REGPARM 4KSTACKS gcc-4.1
parm:           debug:int
parm:           deftaps:int
[root@tvms zaptel]# service zaptel start
Loading zaptel framework:                                  [  OK  ]
Waiting for zap to come online...OK
Loading zaptel hardware modules:No functioning zap hardware found in /proc/zapte
l, loading ztdummy
Running ztcfg:                                             [  OK  ]
[root@tvms zaptel]#
```

> Depending on your compiled kernel modules, the previous screenshot may vary.

## Compiling and installing DAHDI

Follow the steps mentioned here to compile and install the DAHDI kernel module and DAHDI tools.

### Step 1: Compile the kernel module

From within the dahdi-linux module directory, issue the **make** command to compile the kernel module.

```
[root@venus dahdi-linux-2.0.0]# make
make -C /lib/modules/2.6.18-8.1.4.el5/build ARCH=i386 SUBDIRS=/root/dahdi-asterisk/dahdi-linux-2.0.0/drivers/dahdi DAHDI_INCLUDE=/root/dahdi-asterisk/dahdi-linux-2.0.0/include DAHDI_MODULES_EXTRA="" HOTPLUG_FIRMWARE=yes modules DAHDI_BUILD_ALL=m
make[1]: Entering directory `/usr/src/kernels/2.6.18-8.1.4.el5-i686'
  CC [M]  /root/dahdi-asterisk/dahdi-linux-2.0.0/drivers/dahdi/dahdi-base.o
  LD [M]  /root/dahdi-asterisk/dahdi-linux-2.0.0/drivers/dahdi/dahdi.o
  CC [M]  /root/dahdi-asterisk/dahdi-linux-2.0.0/drivers/dahdi/dahdi_dummy.o
  CC [M]  /root/dahdi-asterisk/dahdi-linux-2.0.0/drivers/dahdi/dahdi_dynamic.o
  CC [M]  /root/dahdi-asterisk/dahdi-linux-2.0.0/drivers/dahdi/dahdi_dynamic_loc.o
  CC [M]  /root/dahdi-asterisk/dahdi-linux-2.0.0/drivers/dahdi/dahdi_dynamic_eth.o
  CC [M]  /root/dahdi-asterisk/dahdi-linux-2.0.0/drivers/dahdi/dahdi_transcode.o
  CC [M]  /root/dahdi-asterisk/dahdi-linux-2.0.0/drivers/dahdi/wctdm.o
  CC [M]  /root/dahdi-asterisk/dahdi-linux-2.0.0/drivers/dahdi/wct1xxp.o
```

### Step 2: Install the dahdi kernel module

Once your compilation is completed, issue the **make install** to install your newly-created kernel module.

```
[root@venus dahdi-linux-2.0.0]# make install
make -C /lib/modules/2.6.18-8.1.4.el5/build ARCH=i386 SUBDIRS=/root/dahdi-asteri
sk/dahdi-linux-2.0.0/drivers/dahdi DAHDI_INCLUDE=/root/dahdi-asterisk/dahdi-linu
x-2.0.0/include DAHDI_MODULES_EXTRA=" " HOTPLUG_FIRMWARE=yes modules DAHDI_BUILD
_ALL=m
make[1]: Entering directory `/usr/src/kernels/2.6.18-8.1.4.el5-i686'

  Building modules, stage 2.
  MODPOST
make[1]: Leaving directory `/usr/src/kernels/2.6.18-8.1.4.el5-i686'
build_tools/uninstall-modules dahdi 2.6.18-8.1.4.el5
make -C /lib/modules/2.6.18-8.1.4.el5/build ARCH=i386 SUBDIRS=/root/dahdi-asteri
sk/dahdi-linux-2.0.0/drivers/dahdi DAHDI_INCLUDE=/root/dahdi-asterisk/dahdi-linu
x-2.0.0/include DAHDI_MODULES_EXTRA=" " HOTPLUG_FIRMWARE=yes INSTALL_MOD_PATH= I
NSTALL_MOD_DIR=dahdi modules_install
make[1]: Entering directory `/usr/src/kernels/2.6.18-8.1.4.el5-i686'
  INSTALL /root/dahdi-asterisk/dahdi-linux-2.0.0/drivers/dahdi/dahdi.ko
  INSTALL /root/dahdi-asterisk/dahdi-linux-2.0.0/drivers/dahdi/dahdi_dummy.ko
  INSTALL /root/dahdi-asterisk/dahdi-linux-2.0.0/drivers/dahdi/dahdi_dynamic.ko
  INSTALL /root/dahdi-asterisk/dahdi-linux-2.0.0/drivers/dahdi/dahdi_dynamic_eth
.ko
  INSTALL /root/dahdi-asterisk/dahdi-linux-2.0.0/drivers/dahdi/dahdi_dynamic_loc
.ko
  INSTALL /root/dahdi-asterisk/dahdi-linux-2.0.0/drivers/dahdi/dahdi_echocan_jpa
h.ko
  INSTALL /root/dahdi-asterisk/dahdi-linux-2.0.0/drivers/dahdi/dahdi_echocan_kb1
.ko
  INSTALL /root/dahdi-asterisk/dahdi-linux-2.0.0/drivers/dahdi/dahdi_echocan_mg2
.ko
```

Once your compilation is completed and the kernel module installed, you will be prompted with the following message:

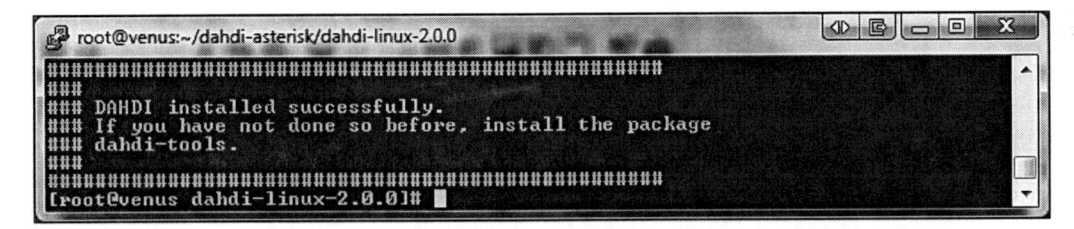

```
###################################################
###
### DAHDI installed successfully.
### If you have not done so before, install the package
### dahdi-tools.
###
###################################################
[root@venus dahdi-linux-2.0.0]#
```

We shall continue with compiling the dahdi-tools package which will allow us to configure and use the dahdi kernel module.

*Installing a 'Vanilla' Asterisk*

## Step 3: Compile the dahdi-tools package

From within the dahdi-tools module directory, issue the **./configure** command to analyze your server and have the compilation script correctly configure your compilation sequence.

## Step 4: Configure the dahdi-tools to be installed

Once the configuration script is completed, issue the `make menuconfig` command to initiate the dahdi-tools configuration menu. The configuration menu will allow you to optimize your dahdi-tools options and compiled utilities.

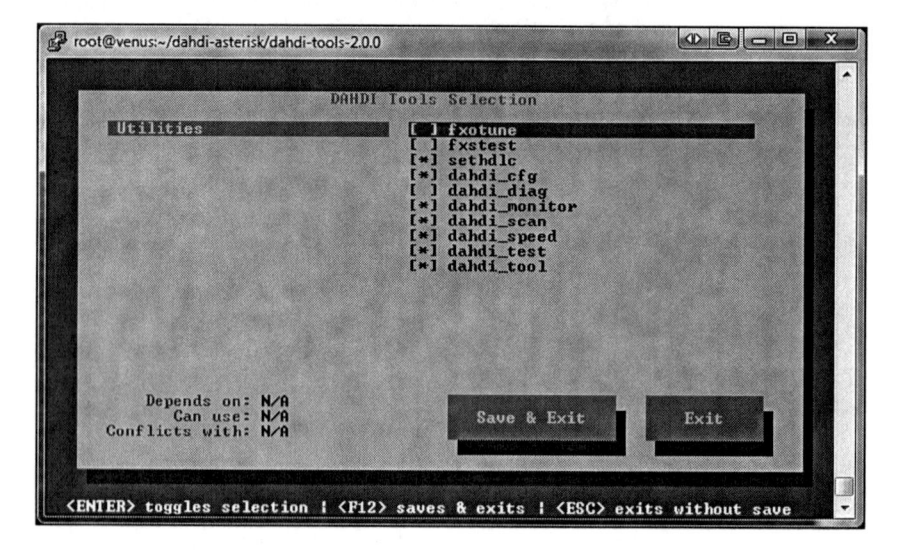

Once you have completed setting your dahdi-tools compilation options, click **Save & Exit** on the configuration menu.

## Step 5: Compile and install dahdi-tools

After saving of the dahdi-tools compilation configuration, issue the **make** command in order to start the compilation of your dahdi-tools.

```
[root@venus dahdi-tools-2.0.0]# make
CC="" CXX="g++" LD="" AR="" RANLIB="" CFLAGS="" make -C menuselect CONFIGURE_SIL
ENT="--silent" makeopts
make[1]: Entering directory `/root/dahdi-asterisk/dahdi-tools-2.0.0/menuselect'
make[1]: `makeopts' is up to date.
make[1]: Leaving directory `/root/dahdi-asterisk/dahdi-tools-2.0.0/menuselect'
make[1]: Entering directory `/root/dahdi-asterisk/dahdi-tools-2.0.0'
CC="" CXX="g++" LD="" AR="" RANLIB="" CFLAGS="" make -C menuselect CONFIGURE_SIL
ENT="--silent" makeopts
make[2]: Entering directory `/root/dahdi-asterisk/dahdi-tools-2.0.0/menuselect'
make[2]: `makeopts' is up to date.
make[2]: Leaving directory `/root/dahdi-asterisk/dahdi-tools-2.0.0/menuselect'
gcc -g -O2 -I. -O2 -g -fPIC -Wall -DBUILDING_TONEZONE    -MD -MT zonedata.lo -MF
 .zonedata.lo.d -MP -c -o zonedata.lo zonedata.c
gcc -g -O2 -I. -O2 -g -fPIC -Wall -DBUILDING_TONEZONE    -MD -MT tonezone.lo -MF
 .tonezone.lo.d -MP -c -o tonezone.lo tonezone.c
gcc -g -O2 -I. -O2 -g -fPIC -Wall -DBUILDING_TONEZONE    -MD -MT version.o -MF .v
ersion.o.d -MP -c -o version.o version.c
gcc -g -O2 -I. -O2 -g -fPIC -Wall -DBUILDING_TONEZONE    -shared -Wl,-soname,libt
onezone.so.1.0 -o libtonezone.so zonedata.lo tonezone.lo version.o -lm
gcc -g -O2 -I. -O2 -g -fPIC -Wall -DBUILDING_TONEZONE    -MD -MT zonedata.o -MF .
zonedata.o.d -MP -c -o zonedata.o zonedata.c
gcc -g -O2 -I. -O2 -g -fPIC -Wall -DBUILDING_TONEZONE    -MD -MT tonezone.o -MF .
tonezone.o.d -MP -c -o tonezone.o tonezone.c
```

Once the installation is completed, simply issue the `make install` command to have your dahdi-tools package installed on your server.

## Differences between Zaptel and DAHDI

While both DAHDI and Zaptel appear to handle the same functionality, their general configuration structure varies slightly—although when examined, it would appear that there are some similarities. The following is a small translation table to assist you in translating the Zaptel and DAHDI file naming conventions and configuration options:

*Installing a 'Vanilla' Asterisk*

| Zaptel filename | DAHDI filename | Description |
|---|---|---|
| `/etc/zaptel.conf` | `/etc/dahdi/system.conf` | The actual configuration file that controls the various aspects of your installed hardware |
| `/etc/sysconfig/zaptel` | `/etc/dahdi/modules` `/etc/dahdi/init.conf` | Shell settings for the runlevel init scripts |
| `/etc/init.d/zaptel` | `/etc/init.d/dahdi` | The kernel module init and configuration init script |

## Compiling and installing libpri

Unlike Zaptel and Asterisk, which require a `./configure` script, the libpri compilation is a straightforward procedure. Compilation is performed using the **make all** command, and installation is performed using the **make install** command.

```
[root@tvms libpri]# make all
gcc -Wall -Werror -Wstrict-prototypes -Wmissing-prototypes -g -fPIC    -c -o q9
31.o q931.c
gcc -Wall -Werror -Wstrict-prototypes -Wmissing-prototypes -g -fPIC    -c -o pr
i_facility.o pri_facility.c
ar rcs libpri.a copy_string.o pri.o q921.o prisched.o q931.o pri_facility.o
ranlib libpri.a
gcc -Wall -Werror -Wstrict-prototypes -Wmissing-prototypes -g -fPIC    -o copy_st
ring.lo -c copy_string.c
gcc -Wall -Werror -Wstrict-prototypes -Wmissing-prototypes -g -fPIC    -o pri.lo
 -c pri.c
gcc -Wall -Werror -Wstrict-prototypes -Wmissing-prototypes -g -fPIC    -o q921.lo
 -c q921.c
gcc -Wall -Werror -Wstrict-prototypes -Wmissing-prototypes -g -fPIC    -o prische
d.lo -c prisched.c
gcc -Wall -Werror -Wstrict-prototypes -Wmissing-prototypes -g -fPIC    -o q931.lo
 -c q931.c
gcc -Wall -Werror -Wstrict-prototypes -Wmissing-prototypes -g -fPIC    -o pri_fac
ility.lo -c pri_facility.c
gcc -shared -Wl,-hlibpri.so.1.0 -o libpri.so.1.0 copy_string.lo pri.lo q921.lo p
risched.lo q931.lo pri_facility.lo
/sbin/ldconfig -n .
ln -sf libpri.so.1.0 libpri.so
ln -sf libpri.so.1.0 libpri.so.1
[root@tvms libpri]# make install
mkdir -p /usr/lib
mkdir -p /usr/include
install -m 644 libpri.h /usr/include
install -m 755 libpri.so.1.0 /usr/lib
if [ -x /usr/sbin/sestatus ] && ( /usr/sbin/sestatus | grep "SELinux status:" |
grep -q "enabled"); then /sbin/restorecon -v /usr/lib/libpri.so.1.0; fi
( cd /usr/lib ; ln -sf libpri.so.1.0 libpri.so ; ln -sf libpri.so.1.0 libpri.so.
1 )
install -m 644 libpri.a /usr/lib
if test $(id -u) = 0; then /sbin/ldconfig -n /usr/lib; fi
[root@tvms libpri]#
```

# Compiling and installing Asterisk

Very much like the Zaptel kernel module, the Asterisk compilation is a four-step operation. While the options available to compile Asterisk from source code are enormous, it is important that you understand the basic idea of fine-tuning your Asterisk installation.

## Step 1: Configure

From within the Asterisk source directory, issue the **./configure** command to have the compilation script scan your system and configure the proper compilation order.

## Step 2: Define the options you would like to compile

Just as with Zaptel, Asterisk (versions 1.4 and onwards) includes a compilation setup and configuration GUI. The GUI enables us to select the Asterisk modules that we would like to compile and install. While it may seem fairly weird to have such a tool, the reason is fairly simple. Asterisk, being primarily a PBX system, includes a multitude of applications and drivers that are usually not required for targeted applications. For example, let's imagine that I build a TDM-to-SIP gateway using Asterisk. There isn't much use for a multi-party conferencing application in such a gateway, now is there?

Each application or driver that is included during the compilation and activation of Asterisk imposes a certain toll on the server running our Asterisk installation. Thus, if we remove modules that are not required, our produced Asterisk toll will be lower than that of a "stock vanilla" Asterisk compilation.

> One could argue that it is possible to disable Asterisk modules that are not required at load time, which would also be true. However, when building a high-performance system, it is always nice to know that you have limited the toll at compile time.

Starting the configuration GUI is performed by issuing the `make menuconfig`, command, to be greeted by the following text based GUI:

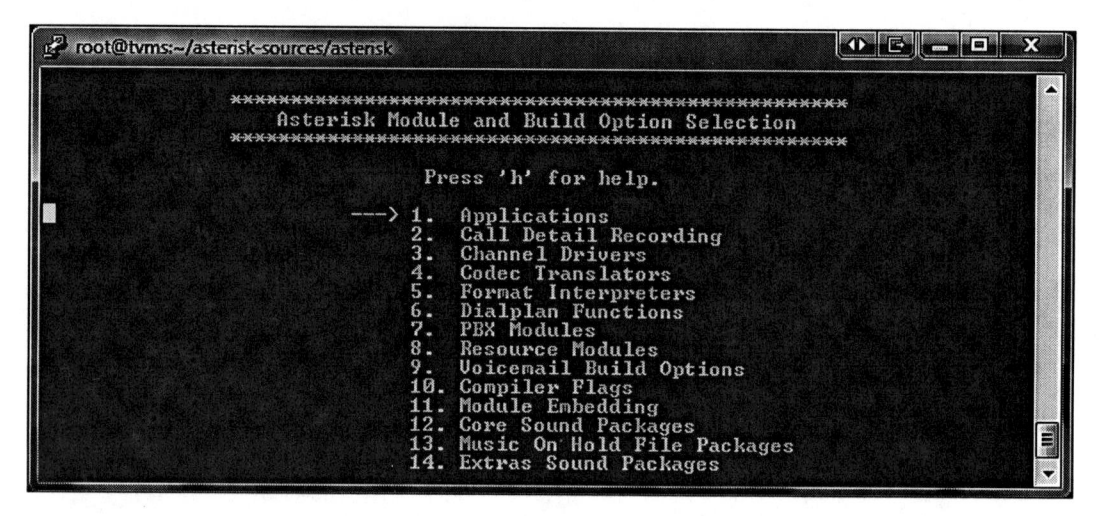

```
**********************************************************
             Asterisk Module and Build Option Selection
**********************************************************
                     Press 'h' for help.
          ---> 1.  Applications
               2.  Call Detail Recording
               3.  Channel Drivers
               4.  Codec Translators
               5.  Format Interpreters
               6.  Dialplan Functions
               7.  PBX Modules
               8.  Resource Modules
               9.  Voicemail Build Options
              10.  Compiler Flags
              11.  Module Embedding
              12.  Core Sound Packages
              13.  Music On Hold File Packages
              14.  Extras Sound Packages
```

As indicated before, there are multitudes of applications and modules that can be included with your Asterisk server. Choosing which ones you require is something that you need to find out on your own. However, we shall take the opportunity to review several sections of this configuration GUI to help you get started.

## Section 1: Applications

As you browse the applications section of the GUI, a description of each application is given at the bottom of the screen. Each application description also includes the dependency (if it exists) of that application. Deciding on your set of applications is crucial, not only from the performance standpoint but also from a security standpoint. For example, imagine that you are now creating an IVR system for dating services. Like any other dating service, the usage of the system in mainly internal, so we don't want to compile a "dial" application that enables our users to dial out of the system (if we had made a mistake in our dialplan or programming). Another good example is the ADSI Programming application, which is used with ADSI-capable phones. If we don't have ADSI-capable phones, there is surely no reason to compile and install this application.

The following image shows the application selection GUI:

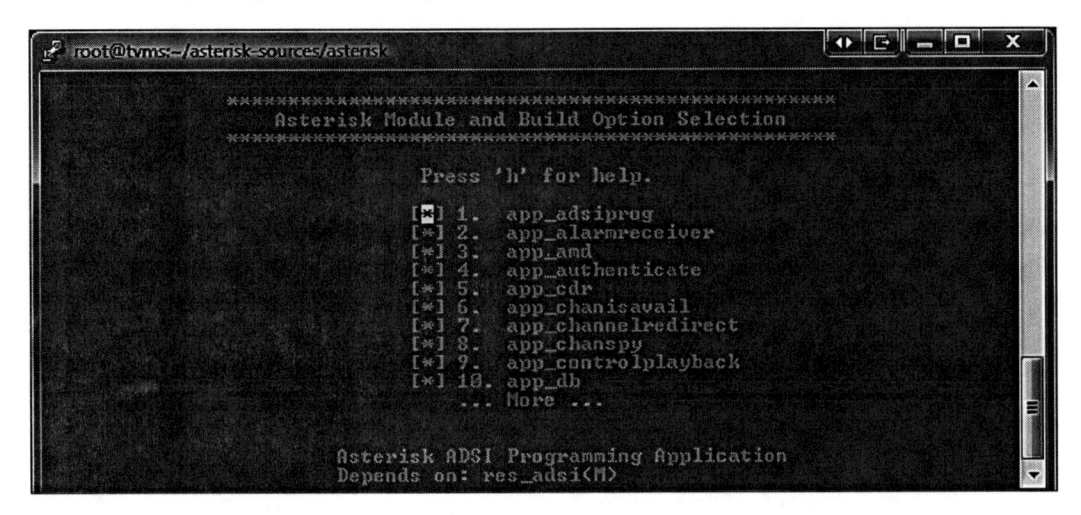

> Even if you decide not to compile a certain application at this point, you can always recompile and install the specific application at a later stage. Don't forget, that we are dealing with a source code — the most flexible way to install a piece of software.

## Section 3: Channel drivers

The channel drivers provide Asterisk's connections to the world, or in layman's terms, the way the calls are passed into and out of Asterisk. When dealing with a development platform, we would usually want to compile all possible channel drivers. However, when dealing with a production environment, this is not always required.

Some people may argue that disabling some channel drivers at compile time in a production environment is a good security practice. This is because Asterisk will not open an unrequired VoIP connection port, and thus, preventing people from either DoS (Denial of Service) attacking your Asterisk system or simply exploiting the exposed channel.

On most systems, you would want to make sure that the following minimal channel driver set is compiled:

| Channel Driver | Description |
| --- | --- |
| chan_iax2 | The Inter Asterisk eXchange protocol used to connect two or more Asterisk servers to one another and provide connectivity to IAX2 capable phones |
| chan_local | A local proxy channel, used in many parts of Asterisk |
| chan_sip | The **Session Initiation Protocol** channel driver, **SIP** is a de-facto industry standard for interconnecting with VoIP providers and various IP phones |
| chan_zap | The Zapata Telephony (Zaptel) channel driver; the Zaptel channel is used with traditional telephony interface, available from Digium, Sangoma and other respective vendors |
| chan_dahdi | The DAHDI channel drivers; this channel driver is identical to chan_zap in terms of its functionality |

At this point, we shall let you explore the compilation GUI yourself and make your own observations. In various sections of this book, we shall do our best to let you explore and find out various things for yourself. Our aim is not only to teach you, but also to expose you to the Asterisk way of thinking, which will help you develop better systems.

## Step 3: Compiling the code

Once you have selected your desired Asterisk module configuration, proceed to the actual compilation. The compilation is performed by issuing the command `make all` from the command line, followed by **make install** in order to install the Asterisk binary executables and shared modules, which is finally followed by `make samples` to install a set of preliminary configuration files.

The following screenshot shows the various completed stages:

```
[CC] recno/rec_search.c -> recno/rec_search.o
[CC] recno/rec_seq.c -> recno/rec_seq.o
[CC] recno/rec_utils.c -> recno/rec_utils.o
[AR] hash/hash.o hash/hash_bigkey.o hash/hash_buf.o hash/hash_func.o hash/hash_log2.o hash/hash_page.o hash/ndbm.o btree/bt_close.o btree/bt_conv.o btree/bt_debug.o btree/bt_delete.o btree/bt_get.o btree/bt_open.o btree/bt_overflow.o btree/bt_page.o btree/bt_put.o btree/bt_search.o btree/bt_seq.o btree/bt_split.o bt ree/bt_utils.o db/db.o mpool/mpool.o recno/rec_close.o recno/rec_delete.o recno/rec_get.o recno/rec_open.o recno/rec_put.o recno/rec_search.o recno/rec_seq.o recno/rec_utils.o -> libdb1.a
[LD] abstract_jb.o acl.o aescrypt.o aeskey.o aestab.o alaw.o app.o ast_expr2.o ast_expr2f.o asterisk.o astmm.o astobj2.o audiohook.o autoservice.o callerid.o cdr.o channel.o chanvars.o cli.o config.o cryptostub.o db.o devicestate.o dial.o dns.o dnsmgr.o dsp.o enum.o file.o fixedjitterbuf.o frame.o fskmodem.o global_datastores.o http.o image.o indications.o io.o jitterbuf.o loader.o logger.o manager.o md5.o netsock.o pbx.o plc.o privacy.o rtp.o say.o sched.o sha1.o slinfactory.o srv.o stdtime/localtime.o strcompat.o tdd.o term.o threadstorage.o translate.o udptl.o ulaw.o utils.o editline/libedit.a db1-ast/libdb1.a -> asterisk
 +------------ Asterisk Build Complete ------------+
 + Asterisk has successfully been built, and       +
 + can be installed by running:                    +
 +                                                 +
 +                  make install                   +
 +-------------------------------------------------+
[root@tvms asterisk]#
```

The preceding screenshot illustrates the completed compilation of the Asterisk source code.

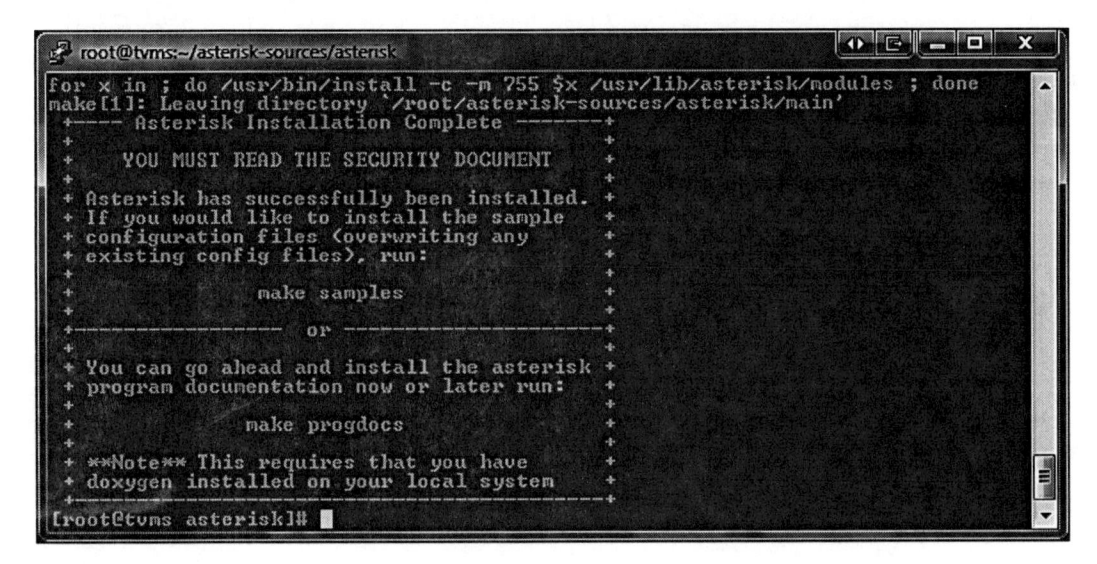

```
for x in ; do /usr/bin/install -c -m 755 $x /usr/lib/asterisk/modules ; done
make[1]: Leaving directory `/root/asterisk-sources/asterisk/main'
 +----- Asterisk Installation Complete --------+
 +                                             +
 +    YOU MUST READ THE SECURITY DOCUMENT      +
 +                                             +
 + Asterisk has successfully been installed.   +
 + If you would like to install the sample     +
 + configuration files (overwriting any        +
 + existing config files), run:                +
 +                                             +
 +                make samples                 +
 +                                             +
 +-------------------- or --------------------+
 +                                             +
 + You can go ahead and install the asterisk   +
 + program documentation now or later run:     +
 +                                             +
 +                make progdocs                +
 +                                             +
 + **Note** This requires that you have        +
 + doxygen installed on your local system      +
 +---------------------------------------------+
[root@tvms asterisk]#
```

This screenshot illustrates the completed installation of the Asterisk binary executables and shared modules. Please note that, at this point your installation lacks sample configuration files and init scripts; so trying to run Asterisk at this point will fail. Issue the **make samples** command in order to create sample configuration files.

*Installing a 'Vanilla' Asterisk*

Once you have completed the sample configuration phase, issue the following command: `asterisk -vvvvcgp`. If a screen similar to the one shown next appears on your console at this point, you have a running Asterisk installation.

```
Asterisk Console on 'tvms.greenfieldtech.net' (pid 2698)
             Added extension '600' priority 2 to ael-demo
             Added extension '600' priority 3 to ael-demo
             Added extension '600' priority 4 to ael-demo
             Added extension '_1234' priority 1 to ael-demo
             Added extension '8500' priority 1 to ael-demo
             Added extension '8500' priority 2 to ael-demo
             Added extension '#' priority 1 to ael-demo
             Added extension '#' priority 2 to ael-demo
             Added extension 't' priority 1 to ael-demo
             Added extension 'i' priority 1 to ael-demo
  [Apr  3 10:02:45] NOTICE[2698]: pbx_ael.c:4114 pbx_load_module: AEL load process
  : compiled config file name '/etc/asterisk/extensions.ael'.
  [Apr  3 10:02:45] NOTICE[2698]: pbx_ael.c:4117 pbx_load_module: AEL load process
  : merged config file name '/etc/asterisk/extensions.ael'.
  [Apr  3 10:02:45] NOTICE[2698]: pbx_ael.c:4120 pbx_load_module: AEL load process
  : verified config file name '/etc/asterisk/extensions.ael'.
  pbx_ael.so => (Asterisk Extension Language Compiler)
        Parsing '/etc/asterisk/cdr_custom.conf': Found
  cdr_custom.so => (Customizable Comma Separated Values CDR Backend)
  Asterisk Ready.
  *CLI> core show version
  Asterisk SVN-branch-1.4-r107714 built by root @ tvms.greenfieldtech.net on a i68
  6 running Linux on 2008-04-03 04:59:16 UTC
  *CLI>
```

Issue the **core show version** command at your Asterisk Command Line interface to show your installed Asterisk version. Please note that your version may vary from the one appearing in the screenshot just shown.

You are probably wondering what the parameters `vvvvcgp` mean. Well, following is the list of the various parameters that the Asterisk binary program (asterisk) will accept as viable parameters for execution:

```
[root@venus dahdi]# asterisk -h
Asterisk 1.4.22, Copyright (C) 1999 - 2008, Digium, Inc. and others.
Usage: asterisk [OPTIONS]
Valid Options:
   -V              Display version number and exit
   -C <configfile> Use an alternate configuration file
   -G <group>      Run as a group other than the caller
   -U <user>       Run as a user other than the caller
   -c              Provide console CLI
   -d              Enable extra debugging
   -f              Do not fork
   -F              Always fork
   -g              Dump core in case of a crash
   -h              This help screen
   -i              Initialize crypto keys at startup
   -I              Enable internal timing if (null) timer is available
   -L <load>       Limit the maximum load average before rejecting new calls
   -M <value>      Limit the maximum number of calls to the specified value
   -m              Mute debugging and console output on the console
   -n              Disable console colorization
   -p              Run as pseudo-realtime thread
   -q              Quiet mode (suppress output)
   -r              Connect to Asterisk on this machine
   -R              Same as -r, except attempt to reconnect if disconnected
   -t              Record soundfiles in /var/tmp and move them where they
                   belong after they are done
   -T              Display the time in [Mmm dd hh:mm:ss] format for each line
                   of output to the CLI
   -v              Increase verbosity (multiple v's = more verbose)
   -x <cmd>        Execute command <cmd> (only valid with -r)
[root@venus dahdi]#
```

# Summary

If you are new to compiling open source software, the actions you have just performed may seem fairly alien to you. Compiling the Asterisk source package is a task most Asterisk developers perform more than once, especially when upgrading Asterisk, or when migrating from one server to another. While some Linux distributions offer pre-compiled versions of Asterisk, it is always a good practice to compile Asterisk from source and get to know how to do this.

# 2
# Basic IVR Development: Using the Asterisk DialPlan

*I am a programmer*–Ken Thompson

Ken Thompson, a Unix Pioneer, refers to himself as a "programmer"—or a developer in other words. Many IVR developers do not regard themselves as programmers. That is a shame as programming an efficient IVR environment using any type of telephony engine requires skill, and when done right can be regarded as a work of art.

> **What is IVR?**
> **IVR** stands for **Interactive Voice Response**, or put in layman's terms, the annoying thing we have to put up with whenever we call the bank or a customer support service.

The development of IVR applications using the Asterisk dialplan configuration language is not difficult. Understanding the concepts of Asterisk's dialplan logic and its utilization are two of the core elements that will be used extensively throughout this book.

> Asterisk's dialplan configuration is available for you via the `extensions.conf` file, available under the `/etc/asterisk` directory.

# The dialplan is a set of "finite state machines"

According to Wikipedia:

> *A finite state machine (FSM) or finite state automaton (plural: automata) or simply a state machine is a model of behavior composed of a finite number of states, transitions between those states, and actions.*

By definition, state machines include the following elements:

| Element | Description |
|---|---|
| An Entry action | The first action executed when entering a state. |
| An Exit action | The last action executed when exiting a state. |
| An Input Action | Performed within a state requiring input from a user or an external source. |
| A Transition Action | Performed when a transition of state is required. |

In the Asterisk world, state machines are actually configuration contexts. The Asterisk dialplan is built of a multitude of configuration contexts, each configuration context containing the logic to be performed in accordance to a dialed number or a dialed pattern.

The following screenshot shows an existing dialplan context, taken from your current configuration:

```
[demo]
;
; We start with what to do when a call first comes in.
;
exten => s,1,Wait(1)                        ; Wait a second, just for fun
exten => s,n,Answer                         ; Answer the line
exten => s,n,Set(TIMEOUT(digit)=5)          ; Set Digit Timeout to 5 seconds
exten => s,n,Set(TIMEOUT(response)=10)      ; Set Response Timeout to 10 seconds
exten => s,n(restart),BackGround(demo-congrats) ; Play a congratulatory message
exten => s,n(instruct),BackGround(demo-instruct)        ; Play some instructions
exten => s,n,WaitExten                      ; Wait for an extension to be dialed.

exten => 2,1,BackGround(demo-moreinfo)      ; Give some more information.
exten => 2,n,Goto(s,instruct)

exten => 3,1,Set(LANGUAGE()=fr)             ; Set language to french
exten => 3,n,Goto(s,restart)                ; Start with the congratulations

exten => 1000,1,Goto(default,s,1)
;
; We also create an example user, 1234, who is on the console and has
; voicemail, etc.
;
:
```

The context name is indicated by the "demo" name that is enclosed in the square brackets. Essentially, the definition **[demo]** directive, simply announces the creation of a new state machine, which will be defined immediately after this directive.

As indicated before, a state machine has an entry action, or in Asterisk's case, a number of entry actions. In order to adapt to Asterisk's dialplan, we shall define a new concept, which will be called "an entry point". The entry point shall be defined as a dialed number or a dialed pattern, associated with a specific set of instructions within the state machine. In the preceding screenshot, we have four distinct entry points: **s**, **2**, **3** and **1000**. The instructions for each entry point are grouped by an **exten** (extension) definition identifying that a group of directives belongs to a specific entry point.

So in accordance with the above, an entry action can be described as the first action performed for a specific extension within a context. The exit action can be described as the last action performed for a specific extension. An input action can be described as an action the reads data from our caller or dialplan, and the traversal between extensions or state machines can be associated with a transition action.

# The dialplan syntax

Asterisk's dialplan is a fairly simplistic, batch-oriented scripting language allowing the IVR developers to rapidly develop IVR applications at ease. Each line in the configuration of an extension looks like this:

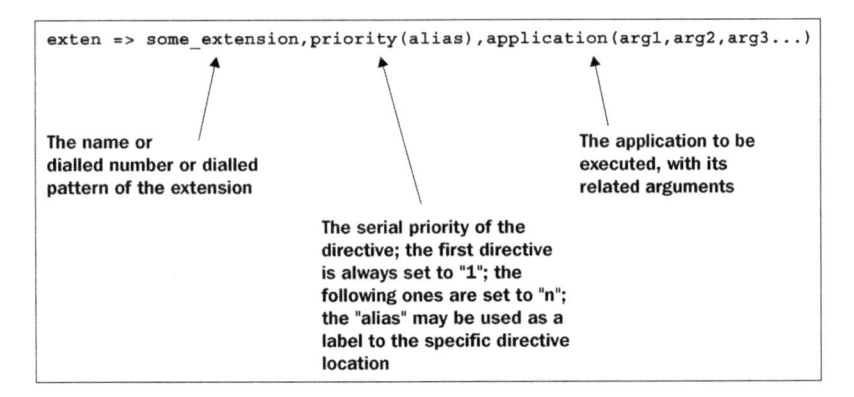

```
exten => some_extension,priority(alias),application(arg1,arg2,arg3...)
```

- The name or dialled number or dialled pattern of the extension
- The serial priority of the directive; the first directive is always set to "1"; the following ones are set to "n"; the "alias" may be used as a label to the specific directive location
- The application to be executed, with its related arguments

# The extension

As we have already mentioned, the extension is invoked according to a dialed number of dialed pattern. As a generalization, this is correct. However, extensions don't have to be numbers; they can also be alpha-numeric characters. In general, the Asterisk dialplan is capable of matching requests to these, by matching the request to the dialplan.

> Asterisk seeks a given context for the dialed extension, starting at the top and working its way to the bottom of the context. The first match in the dialplan is invoked for the dialed number. This means that if you have two extensions that overlap a dialed number, the second one will be made redundant by the first one for that specific dialed number.

## Inclusion of contexts

The following may seem a little complicated, but actually it is not. A given context may include several other contexts. This methodology is generally used to enable a form of modularization within the dialplan. In most cases, we will create contexts that match specific extension numbers and include these into another context. In this manner, we make the specific extension number logic available within the new context.

Including one context within another context is performed by using the following directive:

```
include => context_name
```

This syntax can also be extended to include various time switches, allowing different contexts to be included at specific times:

```
include => daytime|9:00-17:00|mon-fri|*|*
include => nighttime|17:00-9:00|mon-fri|*|*
include => weekend|*|sat-sun|*|*
```

In this example, the daytime context is included from 9am untill 5pm, Monday to Friday, on each day of the month, in every month.

When contexts are included within other contexts, the extension matching changes slightly. First, the master context is searched for the dialed extension. If the extension is not found, Asterisk will search the switches (we will explain switches later on). If the extension is not found in the switches, Asterisk will search each included context.

The dialplan also enables us to include other dialplan configuration files into the existing one. This is usually done to distinguish between various IVR applications running on the same box, and simply allow the developer a means to tidy up. Dialplan file inclusion is performed using the following directive:

```
#include {optional_full_path}dialplan_filename.conf
```

## The [general] and [global] contexts

The `[general]` and `[global]` contexts are used to define global variables to be used throughout the dialplan. In general, the defaults that are installed with your Asterisk distribution are just fine. However, if you want more information about these defaults, we suggest that you look at your default configuration, where the documentation for the `[general]` and `[global]` contexts is available.

## Extension pattern matching

As previously indicated, a dialplan extension (exten) is invoked upon matching either an extension number (or name) or some form of extension pattern. Unlike Unix/Linux based regular expressions, Asterisk dialplan pattern matching is based on a numerical pattern matching facility only, while alphanumeric characters are matched case sensitively.

According to the documentation, Asterisk's pattern matching rules are as follows:

```
; Extension names may be numbers, letters, or combinations
; thereof.  If an extension name is prefixed by a '_'
; character, it is interpreted as a pattern rather than a
; literal.  In patterns, some characters have special meanings:
;
;   X - any digit from 0-9
;   Z - any digit from 1-9
;   N - any digit from 2-9
;   [1235-9] - any digit in the brackets (in this example,
;            1,2,3,5,6,7,8,9)
;   . - wildcard, matches anything remaining (e.g. _9011. matches
;       anything starting with 9011 excluding 9011 itself)
;   ! - wildcard, causes the matching process to complete as soon as
;       it can unambiguously determine that no other matches are
;       possible
;
; For example the extension _NXXXXXX would match normal 7 digit
dialings,
; while _1NXXNXXXXXX would represent an area code plus phone number
; preceded by a one.
```

According to this example, pattern matching is performed from the start of the string (of the left-hand side), going through each character untill we reach the right-hand side. In order to start an extension pattern matching sequence, we use the underscore character (_). For example:

```
exten => _9123X,1,Noop(${EXTEN} was matched)
exten => _9123X,n,SOME_ASTERISK_APPLICATION
```

In this example, we are trying to match any dialed extension of the form 9123 and any one (exactly one) digit that follows. If we were to replace _9123X with _9123XX, we're actually saying that we want to match 9123 followed by any two digits—exactly two so to speak. This is very important, as pattern matching within the dialplan, when carefully planned and configured, can save a whole lot of code later on.

Now, lets talk about the (.) and (!) wildcards. These are used at the right-hand side of the pattern match, usually indicating that we either want to match anything of any length at the end (.) or match when Asterisk is able to determine that it doesn't need to match any more (!). Let's look at the following example:

```
exten => _9123.,1,SOME_ASTERISK_APPLICATION
```

The example basically matches 9123, and anything that follows, of any length or any character. Practically speaking, `_9123.` would match both `912371648131` and `9123NirSimionovich`, as it simply matches everything after the 9123 number.

## Special extensions

Asterisk makes use of some special extensions, which we will explain now:

| Extension | Description |
| --- | --- |
| a | This extension is invoked when a user presses the star key "*" during a voicemail greeting—usually used to allow access to the voicemail system from the outside world |
| h | This extension is invoked when a call is hung up |
| i | This extension is invoked when the user has asked for an invalid extension number in the context |
| o | This extension is called the operator extension and is invoked when the user pressess the zero "0" key from within the voicemail system |
| s | This extension is the start extension, primarily used in situations where an inbound call to a context has no information about the extension number that was dialed (usually associated with Macros and Analog (FXO/FXS) interfaces) |
| t | This extension is invoked upon a user timeout |
| T | This extension is invoked upon an AbsoluteTimeout timer expiration |
| failed | This extension is invoked when an automatic dial-out feature has failed (this will be explained later on in this book) |
| fax | This extension is invoked when a Zap (Analog/Digital) channel has detected a fax signal |
| talk | This extension is invoked by the BackgroundDetect application |

# Dialplan Switches

Switch statements are somewhat of a funky tool. They allow your Asterisk server to query the extensions, available on a remote Asterisk server. Switches are available only for the IAX2 protocol, and are mostly used in conjunction with DUNDI.

> This book doesn't cover DUNDI. If you wish to learn more about DUNDI and various numbering discovery methods, we suggest that you visit the voip-info website, located at http://www.voip-info.org.

Switch statements are formatted as following:

```
switch => IAX2/<username>:[<password>]@<ast_remote>/<context>
```

For example, imagine that a server located at IP address 192.168.0.2 can be accessed via the following IAX2 credentials—username: interpbx, password: contextpbx. Now, the remote server context we'd like the query is named `pbx1_lookup`. So, in our querying server, the following dialplan directive will allow us to query the remote Asterisk server, and if the extension is found in the remote server, route the call to it:

```
switch => IAX2/interpbx:contextpbx@192.168.0.2/pbx1_lookup
```

Switches are a wonderful tool for building large systems, however, be aware that using these requires some careful system planning.

# Variables, applications, and functions

Like any other scripting language, Asterisk's dialplan makes extensive use of variables, applications and functions. We shall now discuss these and the usage of each one.

## Variables—built-in and custom

Variables in Asterisk are commonly referred to as "Channel Variables". However, I would like to distinguish between the two types of channel variables—built-in and custom variables.

Built-in variables are usually associated with either the Asterisk channel itself, or with a specific application. For example, let's take a look at built-in channel variables. Built-in channel variables exist for each channel. These are defined when a channel is created by Asterisk, and are cleared when the channel dies. Here are examples of some built-in channel variables:

- `${CALLERID(all)}`: The current Caller ID name and number

- `${CALLERID(name)}`: The current Caller ID name
- `${CALLERID(num)}`: The current Caller ID number
- `${CHANNEL}`: The current channel name
- `${CONTEXT}`: The name of the current context

These channel variables are available for any active channel and are all accessible from the Asterisk dialplan. You are most probably wondering why some of these have additional information within round brackets, while others don't. Well, this is usually associated with the information carried within the variable. For example, the CALLERID variable may include both a name and a number; so we need a way to access either of the two, or both together.

> Asterisk is a project in a state of constant development and improvement. For an updated list of Asterisk variables, consult the Asterisk community websites. The best location to start would be http://www.voip-info.org/wiki/view/Asterisk+variables.

Custom variables are set by the developer. Setting a variable is very simple, if performed directly from the Asterisk dialplan. Let's examine the following example:

```
exten => _9123X,n,Set(SOME_VAR=3)
exten => _9123X,n,Set(OTHER_VAR=THIS IS A TEST)
```

As you can see, variables can either be numbers or strings—Asterisk can handle both. Accessing a variable from the dialplan is performed using the `${VAR}` directive. For example:

```
exten => _9123X,n,Playback(${SOME_FILENAME})
```

This line of code plays back the audio file, indicated by the SOME_FILENAME variable.

While setting variables is important, it is even more important to be able to manipulate them. Variable manipulation is performed in the same manner as setting the variables—simply by adding the required manipulation. We shall now examine some variable manipulation techniques.

## Mathematical manipulation

The following examples illustrate the use of mathematical manipulations. Each example is followed by a short description:

- For increment:
    ```
    exten => s,1,Set(SOMEVAR=${MATH(${SOMEVAR}+1)});
    ```

- For decrement:
  ```
  exten => s,n,Set(SOMEVAR=${MATH(${SOMEVAR}-1)}) ;
  ```
- For multiplication:
  ```
  exten => s,n,Set(SOMEVAR=${MATH(2*${SOMEVAR})}) ;
  ```
- For division:
  ```
  exten => s,n,Set(SOMEVAR=${MATH(${SOMEVAR}/2)}) ;
  ```

For backward compatibility with a previous version of Asterisk dialplan scripts, the following syntax is also available:

- For increment:
  ```
  exten => s,1,Set(SOMEVAR=$[${SOMEVAR}+1]) ;
  ```
- For decrement:
  ```
  exten => s,n,Set(SOMEVAR=$[${SOMEVAR}-1]) ;
  ```
- For multiplication:
  ```
  exten => s,n,Set(SOMEVAR=$[2*${SOMEVAR}]) ;
  ```
- For division:
  ```
  exten => s,n,Set(SOMEVAR=$[${SOMEVAR}/2]) ;
  ```

## String manipulation

String manipulation is commonly used while manipulating phone numbers and extension numbers. For example, a common practice in telephony is to use various prefixes in order to distinguish between various trunks. However, when a call is made on the trunk, the prefix should either be removed or replaced. This is possible through string manipulation.

## Substrings

Substrings are the most common types of string manipulations in a dialplan script, and we shall make use of these extensively throughout this book. Substrings are extracted using the following syntax: `${variable:offset[:length]}`. The following are some substring examples:

```
exten => s,1,Set(SOMEVAR=${12127773456:1}) ; SOMEVAR = 2127773456

exten => s,n,Set(SOMEVAR=${12127773456:1:3}) ; SOMEVAR = 212

exten => s,n,Set(SOMEVAR=${12127773456:-3}) ; SOMEVAR = 654

exten => s,n,Set(SOMEVAR=${12127773456:-4:3}) ; SOMEVAR = 345
```

## String concatenation

Concatenation of strings is usually performed when you want to pass information from the dialplan to an external source in a single variable (usually Call Detail Records or external applications). The following is an example of a concatenated string:

```
exten => s,1,Set(SOMEVAR=${VAR1}555${VAR2:3})
```

As you can see, this example assigns variable SOMEVAR with the contents of VAR1 followed by the string 555, and the content of VAR2 without the first three characters. You are most probably asking yourself: What is this good for? Well, look at the following example:

```
exten => s,1,Set(SOMEVAR=${VAR1}_${VAR2}_${VAR3}_${VAR4})
```

The example shows that SOMEVAR has been assigned a string containing four different variables, which can be tokenized using the underscore sign (most likely by an external application).

## Variables scoping

Just as with any other scripting/programming language, understanding variable scoping is crucial. Essentially, Asterisk variables are always assigned to their currently active channels, as there is no direct way of accessing variables from one channel to the other.

Bearing this in mind, variable scoping also exists within the Asterisk channel construct itself. Channel-based variable scoping is usually referred to as inheritance in Asterisk terms. **Inheritance** enables us to allow channels that were created from other channels to gain access to variables in the originating channel. For example, let's imagine that a call was made into a specific Asterisk context, and was assigned several variables. At some point, Asterisk will redirect the call into a new context via a local channel driver. We would like to make some of the original variables available to the newly-created local channel.

In order to do so, we need to prefix the variable name with either a single underscore (_) or a double underscore (__). A single underscore will make the variable available to the next channel in line. A double underscore will make the variable available to all the channels that are created from the original channel.

The following is an example:

```
;available to the next channel only
exten => s,1,Set(_NEXT_CHANNEL=12345)
```

```
;available to all the channels that will be created from this oneexten
=> s,n,Set(__ALL_CHANNELS_AFTER_THIS_ONE=67890)

;this is a global variable, available across all channels
Exten => s,n,Set(${GLOBALS(GLOBAL_VAR)}=12345)
```

## Applications and functions

So far, you have learned about contexts, extensions, and variables. It is time to introduce you to the Asterisk application and functions set—the basic building blocks of an Asterisk-based IVR or application.

Asterisk consists of over 150 different applications and over 50 different functions, which when combined into a single extension within a context, will create your IVR application. While applications usually perform an operational function and set various channel variables upon exit, functions operate and manipulate a variable or a string.

> At this point, we will not introduce all of Asterisk's applications or functions as it will be impossible to do so. We shall concentrate our studies from this point onwards on specific applications and functions, with a focus for each episode.

## Your first IVR application

In order to create your first IVR application, we shall assume that you already have one of the following:

- An analog phone connected to your Asterisk server via an analog (FXS) interface
- An analog line connected to your Asterisk server via an analog (FXO) interface
- A digital E1/T1 line connected to your Asterisk server via a PRI interface
- An IP Phone (software/hardware) connected to your Asterisk server via the network

Our first IVR application will perform a simple automatic attendant function designed primarily for an office.

Wikipedia (http://en.wikipedia.org/wiki/Automated_attendant) defines an automatic attendant as:

*In telephony, an automated attendant (also auto attendant or auto-attendant, or sometimes autoattendant or AA) system allows callers to be automatically transferred to a user's extension without the intervention of a receptionist. A receptionist, who acts as the telephone operator, can be reached by pressing 0 on most systems. Although an automated attendant is usually a feature on modern PBX and key phone systems, it is possible to provide one on standard lines and phones.*

While this is only a general definition of what an automatic attendant is, it gives us a fair understanding of what automated attendants do.

Like any other application, we shall now describe our IVR application verbally, and later on via a functional flowchart.

## A simple automatic attendant

Let's describe our automatic attendant:

1. Answer the call.
2. Playback a welcome message.
3. Wait for a key to be pressed (either *1, 2, 3,* or *9*).
4. Repeat steps 2 and 3 thrice, if no key is pressed.
5. If a key is pressed:
    - Any key press will play back a message, followed by a dial in to a preset location.
    - If key pressed is *9*, the call will be disconnected.
6. If no key is pressed, hang up the call.

There is no right or wrong solution when it comes to IVR development—it could either be less optimal or more optimal. The following example illustrates a certain methodology for how to handle the above scenario. However, there may be many other solutions.

## Step 1: Flowchart

Like any other programming project, we shall first start with a detailed flowchart of our automatic attendant.

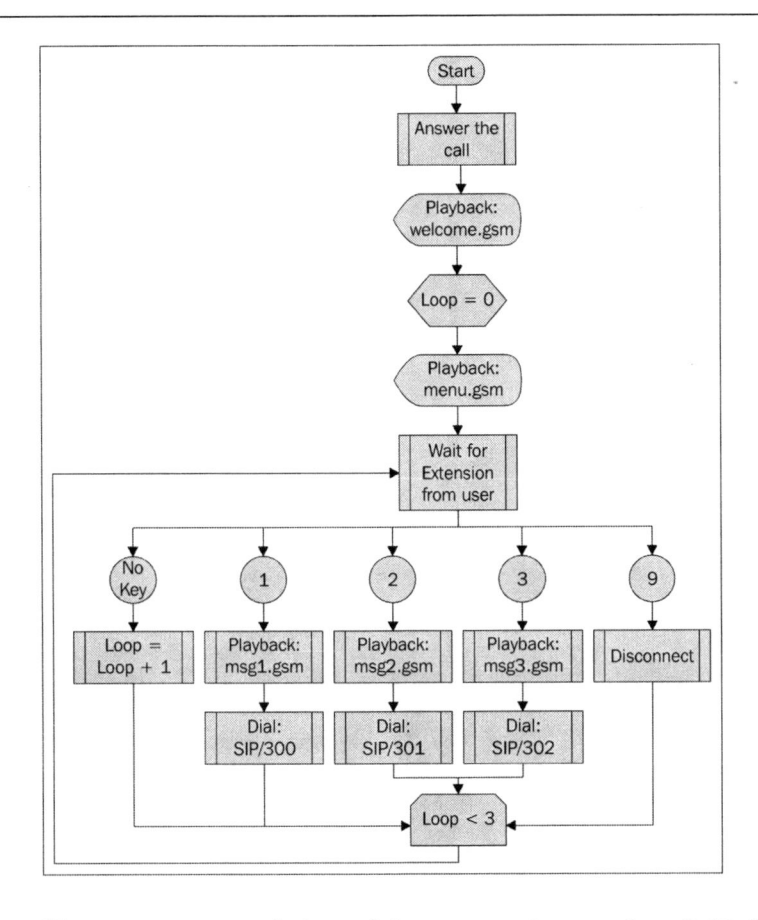

The flowchart illustrates a general view of the automatic attendant. Initially, the attendant will answer the call, which will be followed by an introduction message (indicated by the filename **welcome.gsm**). Further, the welcome message will be followed by an input loop that will repeat thrice if no input is received. Upon receiving input from the user, the attendant will play back a new message (indicated by **msg1.gsm**, **msg2.gsm** and **msg3.gsm**) and will dial a respective SIP channel.

## Step 2: Choice of applications

As we have already indicated, Asterisk includes over 150 different applications and over 50 different functions. However, the question still remains: "Which ones to use?"

We shall now introduce the basic applications that will be used to develop our automatic attendant. Each application is introduced by the Asterisk documentation accompanying the application, followed by additional information (where required).

Basic IVR Development: Using the Asterisk DialPlan

## Application: Answer
### -= Info about application 'Answer' =-

[Synopsis]
Answer a channel if ringing

[Description]
  Answer([delay]): If the call has not been answered, this application will answer it. Otherwise, it has no effect on the call. If a delay is specified, Asterisk will wait this number of milliseconds before returning to the dialplan after answering the call.

## Application: Dial
### -= Info about application 'Dial' =-

[Synopsis]

   Place a call and connect to the current channel

[Description]
  Dial(Technology/resource[&Tech2/resource2...][|timeout][|options][|URL]):
This application will place calls to one or more specified channels. As soon as one of the requested channels answers, the originating channel will be answered, if it has not already been answered. These two channels will then be active in a bridged call. All other channels that were requested will then be hung up.
  Unless there is a timeout specified, the Dial application will wait indefinitely until one of the called channels answers, the user hangs up, or if all of the called channels are busy or unavailable. Dialplan executing will continue if no requested channels can be called, or if the timeout expires.
  This application sets the following channel variables upon completion:
        DIALEDTIME    - This is the time from dialing a channel until
                        when it is disconnected.
        ANSWEREDTIME  - This is the amount of time for actual call.
        DIALSTATUS    - This is the status of the call:
                        CHANUNAVAIL | CONGESTION | NOANSWER | BUSY | ANSWER
                        |CANCEL | DONTCALL | TORTURE | INVALIDARGS
  For the Privacy and Screening Modes, the DIALSTATUS variable will be set to DONTCALL if the called party chooses to send the calling party to the 'Go Away' script. The DIALSTATUS variable will be set to TORTURE if the called party wants to send the caller to the 'torture' script.

This application will report normal termination if the originating channel hangs up, or if the call is bridged and either of the parties in the bridge ends the call.

The optional URL will be sent to the called party if the channel supports it.

If the OUTBOUND_GROUP variable is set, all peer channels created by this application will be put into that group (as in Set(GROUP()=...).

If the OUTBOUND_GROUP_ONCE variable is set, all peer channels created by this application will be put into that group (as in Set(GROUP()=...). Unlike OUTBOUND_GROUP, however, the variable will be unset after use.

Options:

- A(x) - Play an announcement to the called party, using 'x' as the file.
- C - Reset the CDR for this call.
- d - Allow the calling user to dial a 1 digit extension while waiting for a call to be answered. Exit to that extension if it exists in the current context, or the context defined in the EXITCONTEXT variable, if it exists.
- D([called][:calling]) - Send the specified DTMF strings *after* the called party has answered, but before the call gets bridged. The 'called' DTMF string is sent to the called party, and the 'calling' DTMF string is sent to the calling party. Both parameters can be used alone.
- f - Force the callerid of the *calling* channel to be set as the extension associated with the channel using a dialplan 'hint'. For example, some PSTNs do not allow CallerID to be set to anything other than the number assigned to the caller.
- g - Proceed with dialplan execution at the current extension if the destination channel hangs up.
- G(context^exten^pri) - If the call is answered, transfer the calling party to the specified priority and the called party to the specified priority+1.
  Optionally, an extension, or extension and context may be specified. Otherwise, the current extension is used. You cannot use any additional action post answer options in conjunction with this option.
- h - Allow the called party to hang up by sending the '*' DTMF digit.
- H - Allow the calling party to hang up by hitting the '*' DTMF digit.
- i - Asterisk will ignore any forwarding requests it may receive on this dial attempt.
- j - Jump to priority n+101 if all of the requested channels were busy.

## Basic IVR Development: Using the Asterisk DialPlan

k    - Allow the called party to enable parking of the call by sending the DTMF sequence defined for call parking in features.conf.

K    - Allow the calling party to enable parking of the call by sending the DTMF sequence defined for call parking in features.conf.

L(x[:y][:z]) - Limit the call to 'x' ms. Play a warning when 'y' ms are left. Repeat the warning every 'z' ms. The following special variables can be used with this option:

* LIMIT_PLAYAUDIO_CALLER   yes|no (default yes)
  Play sounds to the caller.
* LIMIT_PLAYAUDIO_CALLEE   yes|no
  Play sounds to the callee.
* LIMIT_TIMEOUT_FILE   File to play when time is up.
* LIMIT_CONNECT_FILE   File to play when call begins.
* LIMIT_WARNING_FILE   File to play as warning if 'y' is defined. The default is to say the time remaining.

m([class]) - Provide hold music to the calling party until a requested channel answers. A specific MusicOnHold class can be specified.

M(x[^arg]) - Execute the Macro for the *called* channel before connecting to the calling channel. Arguments can be specified to the Macro using '^' as a delimeter. The Macro can set the variable MACRO_RESULT to specify the following actions after the Macro is finished executing.

* ABORT    Hangup both legs of the call.
* CONGESTION    Behave as if line congestion was encountered.
* BUSY    Behave as if a busy signal was encountered. This will also have the application jump to priority n+101 if the 'j' option is set.
* CONTINUE    Hangup the called party and allow the calling
  party to continue dialplan execution at the next priority.
* GOTO:<context>^<exten>^<priority> - Transfer the call to the specified priority. Optionally, an extension, or extension and priority can be specified.

You cannot use any additional action post answer options in conjunction with this option. Also, pbx services are not run on the peer (called) channel, so you will not be able to set timeouts via the TIMEOUT() function in this macro.

n    - This option is a modifier for the screen/privacy mode. It specifies that no introductions are to be saved in the priv-callerintros directory.

N     - This option is a modifier for the screen/privacy mode. It
        specifies that if callerID is present, do not screen the
        call.
o     - Specify that the CallerID that was present on the *calling*
        channel be set as the CallerID on the *called* channel.
        This was the behavior of Asterisk 1.0 and earlier.
O([x]) - "Operator Services" mode (Zaptel channel to Zaptel
        channel only, if specified on non-Zaptel interface, it
        will be ignored). When the destination answers (presumably
        an operator services station), the originator no longer has
        control of their line.
        They may hang up, but the switch will not release their
        line until the destination party hangs up (the operator).
        Specified without an arg, or with 1 as an arg, the
        originator hanging up will cause the phone to ring back
        immediately. With a 2 specified, when the "operator"
        flashes the trunk, it will ring their phone back.
p     - This option enables screening mode. This is basically
        Privacy mode without memory.
P([x]) - Enable privacy mode. Use 'x' as the family/key in the
        database if it is provided. The current extension is used
        if a database family/key is not specified.
r     - Indicate ringing to the calling party. Pass no audio to the
        calling party until the called channel has answered.
S(x)  - Hang up the call after 'x' seconds *after* the called party
        has answered the call.
t     - Allow the called party to transfer the calling party by
        sending the DTMF sequence defined in features.conf.
T     - Allow the calling party to transfer the called party by
        sending the DTMF sequence defined in features.conf.
w     - Allow the called party to enable recording of the call by
        sending the DTMF sequence defined for one-touch recording
        in features.conf.
W     - Allow the calling party to enable recording of the call by
        sending the DTMF sequence defined for one-touch recording
        in features.conf.

> The Dial application is one of the more complex Asterisk applications, as it provides one of the key features of a PBX—dialing a destination. As you can see, the multitude of options and triggers make up for a fairly complicated command line. Upon finalizing this automatic attendant tutorial, we encourage you to experiment with your automatic attendant by using various Dial triggers.

## Application: Playback
### -= Info about application 'Playback' =-

```
[Synopsis]
Play a file


[Description]
   Playback(filename[&filename2...][|option]):  Plays back given
filenames (do not put extension). Options may also be included
following a pipe symbol. The 'skip' option causes the playback of the
message to be skipped if the channel is not in the 'up' state (i.e. it
hasn't been  answered  yet). If 'skip' is specified, the application
will return immediately should the channel not be
off hook.  Otherwise, unless 'noanswer' is specified, the channel
will be answered before the sound is played. Not all channels
support playing messages while still on hook. If 'j' is specified,
the application will jump to priority n+101 if present when a file
specified to be played does not exist.
This application sets the following channel variable upon completion:
  PLAYBACKSTATUS    The status of the playback attempt as a text
                    string, one of SUCCESS | FAILED
```

## Application: Background
### -= Info about application 'BackGround' =-

```
[Synopsis]
Play an audio file while waiting for digits of an extension to go to.
[Description]
   Background(filename1[&filename2...][|options[|langoverride]
[|context]]): This application will play the given list of files (do
not put extension) while waiting for an extension to be dialed by the
calling channel. To continue waiting for digits after this application
has finished playing files, the WaitExten application should be
used. The 'langoverride' option explicitly specifies which language
to attempt to use for the requested sound files. If a 'context' is
specified, this is the dialplan context that this application will use
when exiting to a dialed extension.  If one of the requested sound
files does not exist, call processing will be terminated.
   Options:
       s - Causes the playback of the message to be skipped
             if the channel is not in the 'up' state (i.e. it
             hasn't been answered yet). If this happens, the
             application will return immediately.
       n - Don't answer the channel before playing the files.
       m - Only break if a digit hit matches a one digit
             extension in the destination context.
```

> The key difference between Playback and Background is that, playback doesn't allow user input to be entered, trapping our user within the playback till it ends. A background-based playback can be interrupted by an extension key press.

## Application: WaitExten
### -= Info about application 'WaitExten' =-

[Synopsis]
Waits for an extension to be entered

[Description]
  WaitExten([seconds][|options]): This application waits for the user to enter a new extension for a specified number of seconds.
  Note that the seconds can be passed with fractions of a second. For example,'1.5' will ask the application to wait for 1.5 seconds.
  Options:
    m[(x)] - Provide music on hold to the caller while waiting for an
             extension. Optionally, specify the class for music on
             hold within parenthesis.

## Application: Hangup
### -= Info about application 'Hangup' =-

[Synopsis]
Hang up the calling channel
[Description]
  Hangup([causecode]): This application will hang up the calling channel. If a causecode is given the channel's hangup cause will be set to the given value.

## Application: SoftHangup
### -= Info about application 'SoftHangup' =-

[Synopsis]
Soft Hangup Application

[Description]
  SoftHangup(Technology/resource|options)
Hangs up the requested channel.  If there are no channels to hangup, the application will report it.
- 'options' may contain the following letter:
     'a' : hang up all channels on a specified device instead of a
           single resource

## Application: EndWhile
-= Info about application 'EndWhile' =-

```
[Synopsis]
End a while loop

[Description]
Usage:  EndWhile()
Return to the previous called While
```

If you have read through the application list provided so far, you are probably thinking about how to create the automatic attendant. We shall now proceed to the final step of the automatic attendant, which is the actual automatic attendant code.

## Step 3: The automatic attendant code

As we've indicated before, we shall create our automatic attendant within a new `extensions.conf` configuration context. We shall name our context as `AutomaticAttendantDemo`. The following is the code for implementing the automatic attendant.

> If you don't recall what _X. means, simply go back to the beginning of this chapter, which deals with pattern matching.

```
[AutomaticAttendantDemo]
exten => _X.,1,Answer    ; Answer inbound calls with 2 or
                         ; more digits extensions
exten => _X.,n,Wait(2)   ; Perform a simple 2 seconds delay
exten => _X.,n,Playback(welcome)
exten => _X.,n,Set(Loop=0)
exten => _X.,n,While($[${Loop} < 3])
exten => _X.,n,Background(menu)
exten => _X.,n,WaitExten(5) ; Wait 5 seconds for user to enter input
exten => _X.,n,Set(Loop=$[${Loop}+1])
exten => _X.,n(LoopEnd),EndWhile()
exten => _X.,n,Hangup()   ; No input from user, so hangup

exten => 1,1,Playback(msg1)
exten => 1,n,Dial(SIP/300,60,rg)
exten => 1,n,Hangup()

exten => 2,1,Playback(msg2)
exten => 2,n,Dial(SIP/301,60,rg)
exten => 2,n,Hangup()

exten => 3,1,Playback(msg3)
exten => 3,n,Dial(SIP/302,60,rg)
exten => 3,n,Hangup()
exten => 9,n,Hangup()
```

```
exten => i,1,Set(Loop=$[${Loop}+1])
exten => i,n,Goto(LoopEnd)
exten => t,1,Set(Loop=$[${Loop}+1])
exten => t,n,Goto(LoopEnd)
```

Our automatic attendant is split into three distinct sections, each one taking care of a different portion of the attendant. We shall now examine each of these sections, explaining them in detail:

### Section 1: The main context body

Our main context body is responsible for answering the inbound call into the context and taking care of our primary attendant functions. The following is the code responsible for the main context body:

```
exten => _X.,1,Answer      ; Answer inbound calls with 2 or
                           ; more digits extensions
exten => _X.,n,Wait(2)     ; Perform a simple 2 seconds delay
exten => _X.,n,Playback(welcome)
exten => _X.,n,Set(Loop=0)
exten => _X.,n,While($[${Loop} < 3])
exten => _X.,n,Background(menu)
exten => _X.,n,WaitExten(5) ; Wait 5 seconds for user to enter input
exten => _X.,n,Set(Loop=$[${Loop}+1])
exten => _X.,n(LoopEnd),EndWhile
exten => _X.,n,softhangup(${CHANNEL} ; No input from user, so hangup
```

As you can see, our first application is set to Answer, which basically answers the call, immediately followed by a two-second waiting period. You are probably wondering what this delay is for? Well, when calls are routed into the context, we don't always know how they were received. In some media types (mainly VoIP), the audio path is not completely established even after the Answer application is invoked. The two-second delay ensures that our audio path is established.

The welcome.gsm file is played using the Playback application.

> Pay attention to the fact that files to be played back are indicated without the .gsm extension. Asterisk is capable of playing files in different formats such as WAV, G.729, ALAW, ULAW, as well as other codecs. This functionality is mainly used for a situation where an inbound call is using a specific codec. Asterisk will try to match the inbound call codec to an existing file in order to reduce the load on the server's CPU by not performing any transcoding to the file played back. Creating the .gsm files for use with Asterisk is possible by converting WAV files to GSM files using the **Linux sox** utility or by using the Windows tools—**NCH Switch**, available from http://www.nch.com.au/switch/.

Following is the welcome message, we enter the main loop indicated by the `While` application. Once inside the loop, our attendant will play back a menu file, followed by a five-seconds waiting period that allows our user to enter an extension number. If the user has not entered an extension within 5 seconds, the loop counter will be increased by one, and the loop will reiterate till, the Loop counter reaches three iterations. If three iterations have been performed, and input has still not been received, the loop will exit and Asterisk will perform a `Hangup` on the `${CHANNEL}`, making it disconnect the dialed call.

## Section 2: Dialed extensions management

The next section handles the various extensions available for the user. Each extension is invoked when a user presses that extension number, while within the `WaitExten` application. The following is the code for that section:

```
exten => 1,1,Playback(msg1)
exten => 1,n,Dial(SIP/300,60,rg)
exten => 1,n,Softhangup(${CHANNEL})

exten => 2,1,Playback(msg2)
exten => 2,n,Dial(SIP/301,60,rg)
exten => 2,n,Softhangup(${CHANNEL})

exten => 3,1,Playback(msg3)
exten => 3,n,Dial(SIP/302,60,rg)
exten => 3,n,Softhangup(${CHANNEL})

exten => 9,1,Softhangup(${CHANNEL})
```

As you can see, we have four distinct extensions defined—1, 2, 3 and 9. If extension 1, 2 or 3 is invoked, our user will be greeted with a specific message, followed by a dialing to a specific SIP device. Upon completion of the call with the SIP device, Asterisk will proceed with the dialplan and disconnect the inbound `${CHANNEL}`.

## Section 3: Error trapping

Just as any computer application, our automatic attendant also requires error trapping. In IVR applications, error trapping refers to situations where the user has entered invalid input, or has not entered any input at all. The following is the code for that section:

```
exten => i,1,Set(Loop=$[${Loop}+1])
exten => i,n,Goto(LoopEnd)

exten => t,1,Set(Loop=$[${Loop}+1])
exten => t,n,Goto(LoopEnd)
```

Our trapping basically traps situations where a user enters a wrong extension (indicated by the `i` extension), or a situation where the user has not entered any input (indicated by the `t` extension).

### Section 4: Debugging

Just as with any other scripting or programming language, debugging the Asterisk dialplan execution is an art. Try following the Asterisk CLI interface as calls traverse your dialplan. Try changing the dialplan to include various errors and examine the output of the CLI regarding your errors.

While Asterisk's CLI messages and behavior can sometimes be a little cryptic (in the worst case, downright undecipherable by humans), the Asterisk CLI is always a good place to start with, when debugging your dialplan.

## Step 4: Testing

At this point, you will be required to point your inbound call or SIP phone to the newly-created context, and simply dial a number to activate it.

# Summary

At this point, you should have a working automatic attendant programmed to your Asterisk installation. Though it is very simplistic and doesn't include a multitude of features, the general concept of developing IVR applications with Asterisk's dialplan language should be clearer at this point.

We would like to send you on a little path of experimentation, which will teach you more about the Dial application—the most complex one for this chapter. Try modifying your automatic attendant to do the following:

- Limit the time of the call to the SIP devices, indicated by in the second section
- Replace the ringing tone with music-on-hold
- Allow both parties to disconnect the call using the * key
- Create a new context and transfer the calling channel and the called channel into that context, causing each channel to dial a new destination automatically

The next chapter will introduce additional tools available to the developer, allowing him/her to develop highly interactive IVR applications.

# 3
# More IVR Development: Input, Recordings, and Call Control

*INPUT! INPUT! Need INPUT!* – Number 5 (Aka: Johnny Five)

If you were born after the year 1986, there is a good chance you are not familiar with John Badham's "Short Circuit" (http://www.imdb.com/title/tt0091949/). In the movie, a malfunctioning robot, known by the designation "Number 5" malfunctions and becomes aware of itself. As it happens, the robot starts learning by absorbing inputs from the environment. While Number 5 tries to obtain "INPUT" from a gas pump (without any success), it remains on the path of obtaining more and more input.

Just like Number 5, an IVR application would not be of much use, without a proper method of allowing user input to traverse into the application. In this chapter, you will learn about the various techniques of interacting with the user. User interaction isn't limited to keypad based input, but also to recording messages from the user, sending output to the user, and controlling the call flow.

## Grabbing and processing user input

In the IVR world, user input is usually associated with DTMF signalling—those funky beeps you hear when you press your phone keypad while on a call.

> **Dual-tone multi-frequency (DTMF)** *signaling is used for telephone signaling over the line in the voice-frequency band to the call switching center. The version of DTMF used for telephone* **tone dialing** *is known by the trademarked term* **Touch-Tone** *(canceled March 13, 1984), and is standardized by ITU-T Recommendation Q.23. Other multi-frequency systems are used for signaling internal to the telephone network.*
>
> *To know more about this, follow this link:* `http://en.wikipedia.org/wiki/DTMF`

Wait a minute! Didn't we process user input already in the previous chapter? Well, not exactly. In the previous chapter, we developed an automatic attendant, which was capable of accepting a user input, and then route a call according to it. User input usually refers to information having no direct relation to our dialplan. The best example would be a bank IVR that asks you to enter your bank account number, and then determines what to do with your call. It would be fairly complicated to handle your bank account information as a dialplan set; we need a better technique here.

## The Read application

The `Read` application enables the IVR developer to play back a preset file to the user, waiting for a certain set of DTMF inputs to be entered. The following is the application documentation:

```
-= Info about application 'Read' =-

[Synopsis]
Read a variable

[Description]
  Read(variable[|filename][|maxdigits][|option][|attempts][|timeout])

Reads a #-terminated string of digits a certain number of times from
the user in to the given variable.

    filename   -- file to play before reading digits or tone with
                  option i
    maxdigits  -- maximum acceptable number of digits. Stops reading
                  after maxdigits have been entered (without requiring
                  the user to press the '#' key).
                  Defaults to 0 - no limit - wait for the user press
                  the '#' key.
                  Any value below 0 means the same. Max accepted value
                  is 255.
    option     -- options are 's' , 'i', 'n'
                  's' to return immediately if the line is not up,
```

```
                'i' to play  filename as an indication tone from your
                indications.conf
                'n' to read digits even if the line is not up.
  attempts      -- if greater than 1, that many attempts will be made in
                the event no data is entered.
  timeout       -- An integer number of seconds to wait for a digit
                response. If greater than 0, that value will override
                the default timeout.

Read should disconnect if the function fails or errors out.
```

> Pay close attention to the last line above: "Read should disconnect if the function fails or errors out". This means that(for example) if you have committed an error in the syntax of the filename, your dialplan will stop and terminate the call.

Let's consider the following example:

```
exten => _X.,n,Read(VAR1,"read_id_number",,,3,5)
```

> You are most probably wondering why there are three consecutive commas in this directive. The reason is that not all parameters to the Read application are mandatory, thus some can simply be discarded.

The dialplan directive just seen will play the file read_id_number back to our user. The file may consist of a message such as "Please enter your ID number, followed by the # key".

We've defined the input to be of any length, so our users can press the # key, or simply timeout on the input. We've not used any of the channel options, as we want our user to come online before entering any information. We're allowing our user up to three attempts, to enter the ID number. This means that the message will be played back, up to three times. The timeout definition defines the waiting time between one input cycle and another, allowing the user to enter inputs up to five seconds after the announcement has ended.

Once the user has entered his/her input sequence, the information entered is stored in the variable indicated, which in our example is VAR1.

> It is imperative to remember that while working with DTMF input, it is almost always entered in the form of digits only. While some directory services allow you to browse the directory according to the first letter of the name, it is usually limited to that. In addition, when creating an IVR application, try your best to refrain from long DTMF input sequences, as these tend to confuse users.

# Branching—Goto, GotoIf, Gosub, and GosubIf

Just as any other programming language, the dialplan scripting language requires the use of branching statements. In other programming languages, such as C, PHP, and PERL, you may know these directives as if-else, switch, and case statements. In the Asterisk world, the equivalents are Goto, GotoIf, Gosub, and GosubIf.

> An Asterisk channel, being a VoIP or TDM channel, can be regarded as a stateful container. This means that once a channel has been established—either by an inbound call or an outbound call—the variables and information associated with the channel will remain accessible for the dialplan as long as the channel is alive. This behavior turns Asterisk into a stateful environment, capable of maintaining multiple instances (channels) of an application operational, without information being crossed from one instance (channel) to another.

As we've seen in the previous chapter, an Asterisk dialplan may include a multitude of configuration contexts, each one capable of performing a predefined number of IVR interactions or operations. In addition, we've also seen that a preset context may use multiple extensions, and we have also already introduced the `while` application, which performs a loop. However, developers can be allowed to branch from outside of a running extension flow to another portion of the execution flow, to another extension, or to another context altogether, which allows them to develop highly complex IVR structures, while maintaining a readable script code.

Let's evaluate a portion of the Asterisk default `extensions.conf` file:

```
[demo]
;
; We start with what to do when a call first comes in.
;
exten => s,1,Wait(1)                        ; Wait a second, just for fun
exten => s,n,Answer                         ; Answer the line
exten => s,n,Set(TIMEOUT(digit)=5)          ; Set Digit Timeout to
                                              5 seconds
exten => s,n,Set(TIMEOUT(response)=10)      ; Set Response Timeout to
                                              10 seconds
exten => s,n(restart),BackGround(demo-congrats)  ; Play a
                                              congratulatory message
exten => s,n(instruct),BackGround(demo-instruct)    ; Play some
                                              instructions
exten => s,n,WaitExten                      ; Wait for an extension
                                              to be dialed.
```

```
exten => 2,1,BackGround(demo-moreinfo)    ; Give some more information.
exten => 2,n,Goto(s,instruct)
exten => 3,1,Set(LANGUAGE()=fr)           ; Set language to french
exten => 3,n,Goto(s,restart)              ; Start with the
                                            congratulations
```

As you can see, we've set some extension directives with aliases (technically referred to by the Asterisk documentation as "labels"—although I prefer the term "aliases"), such as `restart` and `instruct`. If we are going to examine the operational flow of the just seen context, it is fairly clear that Asterisk will perform background playback of two files—`demo-congrats` and `demo-instruct`. This will be followed by Asterisk waiting for the user to enter a new extension to jump to. Let's assume that our user has pressed the digit 3 on his/her keypad, invoking `extension 3`. Let's examine that code:

```
exten => 3,1,Set(LANGUAGE()=fr)           ; Set language to french
exten => 3,n,Goto(s,restart)              ; Start with the
congratulations
```

As you can see, the first line will set a channel variable, the LANGUAGE variable in our case, followed immediately by the `Goto` application. The `Goto` application performs a branching—jumping the execution of the dialplan to the location—indicated by the `Goto` command.

## Goto and GotoIf

Let's now evaluate the `Goto` and `GotoIf` applications:

### -= Info about application 'Goto' =-

```
[Synopsis]
Jump to a particular priority, extension, or context

[Description]
  Goto([[context|]extension|]priority): This application will set
the current context, extension, and priority in the channel structure.
After it completes, the pbx engine will continue dialplan execution
at the specified location.
If no specific extension, or extension and context, are specified,
then this application will just set the specified priority of the
current extension.
  At least a priority is required as an argument, or the goto will
return a -1, and the channel and call will be terminated.
```

> If the location that is put into the channel information is bogus,
> and asterisk cannot find that location in the dialplan, then the
> execution engine will try to find and execute the code in the 'i'
> (invalid) extension in the current context. If that does not exist, it
> will try to execute the 'h' extension. If either or neither the 'h'
> or 'i' extensions have been defined, the channel is hung up, and the
> execution of instructions on the channel is terminated.
> What this means is that, for example, you specify a context that
> does not exist, then it will not be possible to find the 'h' or 'i'
> extensions, and the call will terminate!

### -= Info about application 'GotoIf' =-

> [Synopsis]
> Conditional goto
>
> [Description]
>   GotoIf(condition?[labeliftrue]:[labeliffalse]): This application
> will set the current context, extension, and priority in the channel
> structure based on the evaluation of the given condition. After this
> application completes, the pbx engine will continue dialplan execution
> at the specified location in the dialplan.
> The channel will continue at 'labeliftrue' if the condition is true,
> or 'labeliffalse' if the condition is false. The labels are specified
> with the same syntax as used within the Goto application.  If the
> label chosen by the condition is omitted, no jump is performed, and
> the execution passes to the next instruction.
> If the target location is bogus, and does not exist, the execution
> engine will try to find and execute the code in the 'i' (invalid)
> extension in the current context. If that does not exist, it will try
> to execute the 'h' extension. If either or neither the 'h' or 'i'
> extensions have been defined, the channel is hung up, and the execution
> of instructions on the channel is terminated.
> Remember that this command can set the current context, and if the
> context specified does not exist, then it will not be able to find any
> 'h' or 'i' extensions there, and the channel and call will both be
> terminated!

The Goto application is used to perform an unconditional branch to a preset step in the dialplan. This preset step may be located in the same extension script, in the same context, or in a completely different dialplan context altogether.

The GotoIf application is used to perform an evaluation of variables, thus deciding which priority to jump to. Please note that while Goto is able to branch between contexts and extensions, GotoIf is unable to do so.

Pay special attention to the use of the i and h extensions, which are fairly similar in both the applications. In many IVR cases, when you, as a developer, take your first steps into IVR development with Asterisk, improper handling of these edge cases can cause your application to sporadically hang up, leaving you baffled and confused as to what happened.

# Writing expressions

When using the `GotoIf` directive or any other application that uses expressions, it is important to use the correct syntax. Unlike a compiled language, Asterisk won't really complain if the expression appearing in the dialplan is wrong. However, the results of the expression cannot usually be foreseen.

Evaluating expressions is performed using the following format:

```
$[expr1 operator expr2]
```

Basically, the `$[]` operator tells Asterisk, which of the expressions that appear within these brackets need to be evaluated. Let's examine some evaluations:

| Expression | Explanation |
|---|---|
| `$[${CALLERID(num)} = 123456]` | This expression evaluates the caller ID number, associated with the current channel |
| `$[${CALLERID(name)} = "Simon"]` | This evaluation will return a constant false value, as its syntax is incorrect. In order to indicate to Asterisk that we want to evaluate strings, we must use the quotes indication with the variable name |
| `$["${CALLERID(name)}" = "Simon"]` | This is the correct form of the previous evaluation |

Asterisk makes usage of several operators while writing expressions. The following is a list of available operators:

## Logical operators

Let's turn our attention to the logical operators.

- `expr1 | expr2` (Logical OR)

    If expr1 evaluates to a non-empty string or a non-zero value, "true" value is returned. Otherwise, the evaluation of expr2 is returned.

- `expr1 & expr2` (Logical AND)

    If both the expressions evaluate to non-empty strings or non-zero values, then value "1" (true) is returned, else "0" (false) is returned.

- `!expr` (Logical Unary Complement)

    There should'nt be a space between the '!' and the expression, else an error will occur.

## Comparison operators

Now we will see the comparison operators.

- `expr1 = expr2`
- `expr1 != expr2`
- `expr1 < expr2`
- `expr1 > expr2`
- `expr1 <= expr2`
- `expr1 >= expr2`

If both the arguments are integers, the result of an integer comparison is returned. Otherwise, the result of string comparison is returned using the locale-specific collation sequence. In either case, the result of a comparison is 1 if the specified relation is true or 0 if the relation is false.

## Arithmetic operators

The following are arithmetic operators.

- `expr1 + expr2`
- `expr1 - expr2`
- `- expr` (unary negation operator)

Return the results of addition or subtraction of integer-valued arguments.

- `expr1 * expr2`
- `expr1 / expr2`
- `expr1 % expr2`

Return the results of multiplication, integer division, or the remainder of the integer-valued arguments.

## Regular expressions

Asterisk allows the use of regular expressions within the dialplan. While the regular expressions are not an integral part of this book, we include an example here that may assist you in writing regular expressions of your own.

```
exten => stripcidtext,n,Set(regx="([0-9]+)")
; Note the quotes -- and note that parentheses are REQUIRED if you
; want to return the matched string

exten => stripcidtext,n,Set(cid2=$["${cid}" : ${regx}])
; Returns numeric beginning to string
```

## Operator precedence

Just as any other programming language, operators follow a certain order of precedence. The following are the precedence rules for Asterisk's operators:

1. Parentheses — ( )
2. Unary operators — !, -
3. Regular expression comparison — :, =~
4. Multiplicative arithmetic operators — *, /, %
5. Additive arithmetic operators — +, -
6. Comparison operators — =, !=, <, >, <=, >=
7. Logical operators — |, &
8. Conditional operator — ? :

> This information is taken from the Asterisk wiki, located at http://www.voip-info.org/wiki/index.php?page=Asterisk+Expressions

## Gosub and GosubIf

When you were new to the programming world, your first programming language would have been either Pascal or — if you were unlucky — Java. For those of us who are over thirty years old, our first programming language would have been Basic. While Basic was a very simplistic and batch-oriented computer language, the dreaded `Gosub` directive was always a case where our program would start doing things we didn't really plan. Asterisk's `Gosub` and `GosubIf` directives are fairly similar.

```
-= Info about application 'Gosub' =-

[Synopsis]
Jump to label, saving return address
[Description]
Gosub([[context|]exten|]priority)
   Jumps to the label specified, saving the return address.

   -= Info about application 'GosubIf' =-

[Synopsis]
Conditionally jump to label, saving return address

[Description]
GosubIf(condition?labeliftrue[:labeliffalse])
   If the condition is true, then jump to labeliftrue.  If false,
jumps to labeliffalse, if specified.  In either case, a jump saves the
return point in the dialplan, to be returned to with a Return.
```

As you can see, the main difference between the two directives is that `GosubIf` enables us to branch into our subroutine using an evaluation. Unlike the `Goto` directive, the `Gosub` directive has the ability to save the location that we branched from, and return to the next step in sequence. This enables new functionality, especially in modularizing our dialplan code.

Let's examine what a dialplan would look like:

```
exten => _XXXX,1,Gosub(setcid)
exten => _XXXX,n,Dial(Zap/g1/00${EXTEN})
exten => _XXXX,n,Congestion
exten => _XXXX,n(setcid),SetCALLERID(all)=Movie Phone <12127773456>)
exten => _XXXX,n,Return
```

Essentially, the above dialplan extract doesn't do anything interesting. It simply seeks a dialed extension that has exactly four digits in it, performs a `Gosub` to the `setcid` subroutine, followed by a `Dial` directive. The `Gosub` directive specifies that the dialplan forks to the `setcid` label, performs the subroutine, and resumes at the next step.

Let's examine the `setcid` subroutine:

```
exten => _XXXX,n(setcid),SetCALLERID(all)=Movie Phone <12127773456>)
exten => _XXXX,n,Return
```

> In a similar fashion, the `GoSub` and `GoSubIf` directive are also able to activate subroutines in different contexts from the currently running one.

As you can see, the subroutine simply sets the caller ID information and then returns back to the main extension loop, immediately followed by dialing our TDM group—g1.

Let's examine a more complex example:

```
[moviephone-main-ivr]
exten => 12127773456,1,Answer
exten => 12127773456,n,Wait(1)
exten => 12127773456,n,Read(menu,moviephone_menu,1,,3,5)
exten => 12127773456,n,Gosub(moviephone-checkmenu,${EXTEN},1)
exten => 12127773456,n,Congestion()

[moviephone-checkmenu]
exten => _X.,1,GotoIf($[${menu} == 1]?menu_1)
exten => _X.,n,GotoIf($[${menu} == 2]?menu_2)
exten => _X.,n,GotoIf($[${menu} == 3]?menu_3)
exten => _X.,n,GotoIf($[${menu} == 4]?menu_4)
```

```
exten => _X.,n,GotoIf($[${menu} == 5]?menu_5)
exten => _X.,n,Return()
exten => _X.,n(menu_1),Goto(moviephone-menu1,${EXTEN},1)
exten => _X.,n(menu_2),Goto(moviephone-menu2,${EXTEN},1)
exten => _X.,n(menu_3),Goto(moviephone-menu3,${EXTEN},1)
exten => _X.,n(menu_4),Goto(moviephone-menu4,${EXTEN},1)
exten => _X.,n(menu_5),Goto(moviephone-menu5,${EXTEN},1)
```

The above example basically answers the call and plays back a welcome menu, waiting for our user to enter a single digit input. Once the input is received, Asterisk will invoke the subroutine `movie-checkmenu` that will check the user's input. If the input doesn't match anything, the subroutine returns and the call is terminated with a congestion sound.

## Exec, ExecIf, and TryExec

Let's now evaluate the `Exec`, `ExecIf`, and `TryExec` applications now:

```
-= Info about application 'Exec' =-

[Synopsis]
Executes dialplan application

[Description]
Usage: Exec(appname(arguments))
  Allows an arbitrary application to be invoked even when not
hardcoded into the dialplan.  If the underlying application
terminates the dialplan, or if the application cannot be found,
Exec will terminate the dialplan.
  To invoke external applications, see the application System.
  If you would like to catch any error instead, see TryExec.
  -= Info about application 'ExecIf' =-
[Synopsis]
Executes dialplan application, conditionally

[Description]
Usage:  ExecIF (<expr>|<app>|<data>)
If <expr> is true, execute and return the result of <app>(<data>).
If <expr> is true, but <app> is not found, then the application
will return a non-zero value.
```

### -= Info about application 'TryExec' =-

```
[Synopsis]
Executes dialplan application, always returning

[Description]
Usage: TryExec(appname(arguments))
   Allows an arbitrary application to be invoked even when not
hardcoded into the dialplan. To invoke external applications
see the application System.  Always returns to the dialplan.
The channel variable TRYSTATUS will be set to:
     SUCCESS    if the application returned zero
     FAILED     if the application returned non-zero
     NOAPP      if the application was not found or was not specified
```

You are most probably asking yourself: "I can understand why I would like to use the ExecIf application. Yes, it is quite useful, but why would I use Exec?" Well, the Exec application is a way for you to run different applications via a single Asterisk dialplan extension directive.

Let's evaluate the following dialplan:

> The following dialplan includes an advanced directive—AGI. While the AGI directive is discussed in the next chapter, regard it as an application that accepts data, manipulates it, and returns a variable or set of variables to the operational channel.

```
[moviephone-mainmenu]
exten => _X.,1,Read(menuselect,mainmenu,1,,3,5)
exten => _X.,n,AGI(CheckMenuInput.agi)
exten => _X.,n,Exec(${menuapp_name},${menuapp_params})
```

The dialplan just seen reads a DTMF signal from the user, followed by an activation of an external AGI script. The purpose of our AGI scripts is simply to check which DTMF was keyed, and accordingly set the two environment variables—${menuapp_name} and ${menuapp_params}. This means that our little dialplan can execute any Asterisk application, simply by keying in a different number at the main menu.

> The above methodology is fairly common with dynamic IVR structures, and can be extended to include various external communication structures such as XML-RPC, SOAP, and WSDL among others.

Let's examine the same functionality, however, this time using the
`ExecIf` application:

```
[moviephone-mainmenu]
exten => _X.,1,Read(menuselect,mainmenu,1,,3,5)
exten => _X.,n,ExecIf($[${menuselect} == 1],playback,sound1)
exten => _X.,n,ExecIf($[${menuselect} == 2],background,sound2)
exten => _X.,n,ExecIf($[${menuselect} == 3],Goto,submenu,${EXTEN},1)
```

This code accomplishes a task similar to the previous one. However, our code is less dynamic and highly rigid. Opting for one over another doesn't make sense as each one is used in a different scenario. It is up to you to use these accordingly.

# Macros—Macro and MacroExclusive

Macros enable the developer to develop small dialplan contexts to perform specific functions, for example, processing some information and then returning to the place they were called from. Following is an example of a dialplan macro:

```
[macro-example];
;    ${ARG1} - The destination to call
;    ${ARG2} - How long to call the destination
;    ${ARG3} - Parameters to the dial command
;
exten => s,1,Dial(${ARG1},${ARG2},${ARG3})
exten => s,n,Goto(s-{DIALSTATUS},1)
exten => s,n,MacroExit

exten => s-NOANSWER,1,Playback(there_was_no_answer)
exten => s-NOANSWER,n,MacroExit

exten => s-BUSY,1,Playback(the_destination_is_busy)
exten => s-BUSY,n,MacroExit

exten => _s-.,1,Playback(an_error_occured)
exten => _s-.,n,MacroExit
```

Ok, the just seen example is fairly simplistic for a macro, however, it provides a very nice example. The above macro is used as a dialing handler, or to be more precise, a dialer handler with error handling. When a macro is invoked, it automatically invokes the s extension. Once the s extension is invoked, execution is performed exclusively within the macro.

> If you decide to branch from your macro back to the main dialplan by using `Goto`, `GotoIf` or other branching techniques, your macro will exit at that point.

Execution of a Macro from the dialplan is performed according to the following:

```
exten => 1234,1,Macro(example,SIP/1234,120,r)
```

In our example, we execute the `example` macro with the destination set to `SIP/1234`, the timeout to `120` seconds, and the parameters set to `r`.

Macros provide information regarding where the macro was called from, while at the same time, provide the ability to return to a specific offset in the context that called the macro. These are available through the following variables:

| Variable name | Details |
| --- | --- |
| ${MACRO_EXTEN} | The extension from which the macro was invoked |
| ${MACRO_CONTEXT} | The context from which the macro was invoked |
| ${MACRO_PRIORITY} | The priority, in the extension dialplan, from which the macro was invoked |
| ${MACRO_OFFSET} | When returning from the macro to ${MACRO_PRIOTIRY}@${MACRO_EXTEN}@${MACRO_CONTEXT}, return to the priority designated by ${MACRO_PRIORITY}+1+${MACRO_OFFSET} |

> While the ${MACRO_OFFSET} variable exists, I urge you to refrain from using it often, as it will make your dialplans fairly complex to read and debug. If you really need to return to a specific offset, consider returning a value to the macro calling context, and then branching according to that.

> If you execute the Background application within a context, you would expect that pressing a key while Background is executed will pass the control to the extension that was entered while Background was running. Well, this is not true. This will cause a jump back to the macro calling context and will seek the extension keyed in the original macro calling context.

> Version Notice: The Macro application has been in the Asterisk code since its first version. But the GoSub application, after its introduction in Asterisk 1.6, is now the prefrered method of performing this functionality

Another way of executing a macro is using the MacroExclusive application. The purpose of MacroExclusive is to restrict the execution of a macro to a single channel at a time. All other channels will have to wait till the first channel frees the macro. This was mainly created as a means of providing a way to lock the usage of a macro, thereby allowing the synchronization of database manipulations and global variables in Asterisk.

## Additional Asterisk applications

At this point, we shall introduce you to some new Asterisk applications. However, we won't go into the functionality of each application. These applications are being introduced to you at this point, in order to encourage you to experiment and try new applications as you go along.

### -= Info about application 'Busy' =-

```
[Synopsis]
Indicate the Busy condition

[Description]
  Busy([timeout]): This application will indicate the busy condition
to the calling channel. If the optional timeout is specified, the
calling channel will be hung up after the specified number of seconds.
Otherwise, this application will wait until the calling channel
hangs up.
```

### -= Info about application 'Congestion' =-

```
[Synopsis]
Indicate the Congestion condition

[Description]
  Congestion([timeout]): This application will indicate the congestion
condition to the calling channel. If the optional timeout is
specified, the calling channel will be hung up after the specified
number of seconds.
Otherwise, this application will wait until the calling channel
hangs up.
```

> **Congestion** refers to a situation where you are trying to call a specific destination, via a specific route (be it TDM of VoIP) and received back an indication that there are no more lines available. In older PBX systems, this would generate a specific tone — known as the congestion tone. The Congestion application generates that tone to the connected channel, directly from the dialplan.

## -= Info about application 'ControlPlayback' =-

[Synopsis]
Play a file with fast forward and rewind

[Description]

   ControlPlayback(file[|skipms[|ff[|rew[|stop[|pause[|restart|options]]]]]]]):
This application will play back the given filename. By default, the '*' key
can be used to rewind, and the '#' key can be used to fast-forward.
Parameters:
  skipms   - This is number of milliseconds to skip when rewinding or
             fast-forwarding.
  ff       - Fast-forward when this DTMF digit is received.
  rew      - Rewind when this DTMF digit is received.
  stop     - Stop playback when this DTMF digit is received.
  pause    - Pause playback when this DTMF digit is received.
  restart  - Restart playback when this DTMF digit is received.
Options:
  j - Jump to priority n+101 if the requested file is not found.
This application sets the following channel variable upon completion:
    CPLAYBACKSTATUS -  This variable contains the status of the attempt
                             as a text string, one of: SUCCESS | USERSTOPPED
                             | ERROR

## -= Info about application 'SayAlpha' =-

[Synopsis]
Say Alpha

[Description]
  SayAlpha(string): This application will play the sounds that correspond to the letters of the given string.

## -= Info about application 'SayDigits' =-

[Synopsis]
Say Digits

[Description]
  SayDigits(digits): This application will play the sounds that correspond to the digits of the given number. This will use the language that is currently set for the channel. See the LANGUAGE function for more information on setting the language for the channel.

## -= Info about application 'SayNumber' =-

[Synopsis]
Say Number

[Description]
  SayNumber(digits[,gender]): This application will play the sounds that correspond to the given number. Optionally, a gender may be specified.
This will use the language that is currently set for the channel. See the LANGUAGE function for more information on setting the language for the channel.

## -= Info about application 'Monitor' =-

[Synopsis]
Monitor a channel

[Description]
Monitor([file_format[:urlbase]|[fname_base]|[options]]):
Used to start monitoring a channel. The channel's input and output voice packets are logged to files until the channel hangs up or monitoring is stopped by the StopMonitor application.
   file_format     optional, if not set, defaults to "wav"
   fname_base      if set, changes the filename used to the one
                   specified.
   options:
     m   - when the recording ends mix the two leg files into one and
           delete the two leg files.  If the variable MONITOR_EXEC is
           set, the application referenced in it will be executed
           instead of soxmix and the raw leg files will NOT be deleted
           automatically.
           soxmix or MONITOR_EXEC is handed 3 arguments, the two leg
           files and a target mixed file name which is the same as the
           leg file names only without the in/out designator.
           If MONITOR_EXEC_ARGS is set, the contents will be passed on
           as additional arguements to MONITOR_EXEC
           Both MONITOR_EXEC and the Mix flag can be set from the
           administrator interface
     b   - Don't begin recording unless a call is bridged to
           another channel

Returns -1 if monitor files can't be opened or if the channel is already monitored, otherwise 0.

### -= Info about application 'StopMonitor' =-

[Synopsis]
Stop monitoring a channel

[Description]
StopMonitor
Stops monitoring a channel. Has no effect if the channel is not
monitored

### -= Info about application 'MixMonitor' =-

[Synopsis]
Record a call and mix the audio during the recording

[Description]
   MixMonitor(<file>.<ext>[|<options>[|<command>]])

Records the audio on the current channel to the specified file.
If the filename is an absolute path, uses that path, otherwise
creates the file in the configured monitoring directory from
asterisk.conf.

Valid options:
    a       - Append to the file instead of overwriting it.
    b       - Only save audio to the file while the channel is bridged.
              Note: Does not include conferences or sounds played to
              each bridged party.
    v(<x>)  - Adjust the heard volume by a factor of <x> (range -4 to 4)
    V(<x>)  - Adjust the spoken volume by a factor of <x> (range -4 to 4)
    W(<x>)  - Adjust the both heard and spoken volumes by a factor of <x>
              (range -4 to 4)
<command> will be executed when the recording is over
Any strings matching ^{X} will be unescaped to ${X}.
All variables will be evaluated at the time MixMonitor is called.
The variable MIXMONITOR_FILENAME will contain the filename used to
record.

### -= Info about application 'StopMixMonitor' =-

[Synopsis]
Stop recording a call through MixMonitor

[Description]
   StopMixMonitor()
Stops the audio recording that was started with a call to MixMonitor()
on the current channel.

**-= Info about application 'MusicOnHold' =-**

```
[Synopsis]
Play Music On Hold indefinitely

[Description]
MusicOnHold(class): Plays hold music specified by class.  If omitted,
the default music source for the channel will be used. Set the default
class with the SetMusicOnHold() application.
Returns -1 on hangup.
Never returns otherwise.
```

## Self exploration

At this point, we would like to send you on a journey of self-exploration, using the applications and methodologies you've learned so far. Using the same automatic attendant dialplan from Chapter 1, extend the dialplan code to include the following new features:

- Add music-on-hold features to each of the extensions dialled, to be played back untill the extension is picked up
- Add recording of the call to some of your extensions
- Change the main body of the automatic attendant to use the Read application instead of using the Background application

## Summary

At this point, you should be able to develop the IVR application in a manner that is slightly more complicated than the applications we've discussed in Chapter 2. The introduction of the Read application, and the conditional branching and execution, enable new flexibility that was not available in Chapter 1. From this point onwards, the journey becomes more and more complicated as we go along. So take a break at this point, grab a cup of coffee, and relax.

# 4
# A Primer to AGI: Asterisk Gateway Interface

*Explanation separates us from astonishment, which is the only gateway to the incomprehensible.* –Eugene Ionesco

Eugene Ionesco, a Romanian/French playwright and dramatist is known mostly for his work on the "Theatre of the Absurd". Asterisk **AGI (Asterisk Gateway Interface)** enables an IVR developer to develop IVR structures that are sometimes, bordering on the absurd, as applications tend to become more and more complex by using AGI. However, there are some scenarios where common dialplan practices are no longer applicable, and the use of an external logic is a must. Enter AGI!

## How does AGI work?

Let's examine the following diagram:

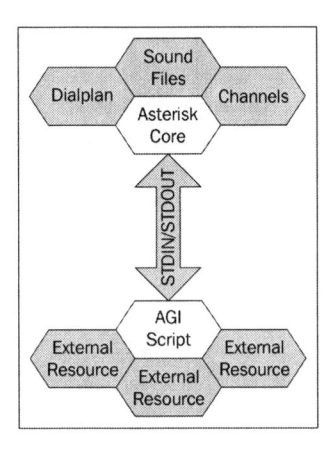

As the previous diagram illustrates, an AGI script communicates with Asterisk via two standard data streams—STDIN (Standard Input) and STDOUT (Standard Output). From the AGI script point-of-view, any input coming in from Asterisk would be considered STDIN, while output to Asterisk would be considered as STDOUT.

The idea of using STDIN/STDOUT data streams with applications isn't a new one, even if you're a junior level programmer. Think of it as regarding any input from Asterisk with a read directive and outputting to Asterisk with a print or echo directive. When thinking about it in such a simplistic manner, it is clear that AGI scripts can be written in any scripting or programming language, ranging from BASH scripting, through PERL/PHP scripting, to even writing C/C++ programs to perform the same task.

Let's now examine how an AGI script is invoked from within the Asterisk dialplan:

```
exten => _X.,1,AGI(some_script_name.agi,param1,param2,param3)
```

As you can see, the invocation is similar to the invocation of any other Asterisk dialplan application. However, there is one major difference between a regular dialplan application and an AGI script—the resources an AGI script consumes. While an internal application consumes a well-known set of resources from Asterisk, an AGI script simply hands over the control to an external process. Thus, the resources required to execute the external AGI script are now unknown, while at the same time, Asterisk consumes the resources for managing the execution of the AGI script. Now, imagine that your script is written in BASH. This means that every time you run an AGI script, a full BASH shell is invoked for the script. Ok, so BASH isn't much of a resource hog, but what about Java? This means that the choice of programming language for your AGI scripts is important. Choosing the wrong programming language can often lead to slow systems and in most cases, non-operational systems.

While one may argue that the underlying programming language has a direct impact on the performance of your AGI application, it is imperative to learn the impact of each. To be more exact, it's not the language itself, but more the technology of the programming language runtime that is important. The following table tries to distinguish between three programming languages' families and their applicability to AGI development.

| Language Family | Member Languages | Details |
| --- | --- | --- |
| Binary Compiled | C, C++, Pascal | The executable code generated can be highly optimized; thus, its general system footprint is fairly light; although these are the perfect choice for AGI development, the development process is long and tedious |
| Virtual Machine | Java, C#, Mono | Virtual machine executables incur a hefty toll, with the virtual machine itself usually consuming much memory; while languages like Java enable rapid development, their main use should be limited to FastAGI (described later in this book) |
| Interpreted | PERL, PHP, Python, Ruby | Interpreted languages have a slightly higher toll than binary compiled executables; however, their general footprint is much smaller than that of the Virtual Machine based languages; Interpreted languages, such as PHP, make up for about 80% of the AGI development in the world, and easily fit both AGI and FastAGI development |

# EAGI, DeadAGI and FastAGI

AGI has three cousins—EAGI, DeadAGI, and FastAGI. We shall now explain the use of each of these variants, and their proper usage.

## EAGI—Enhanced Asterisk Gateway Interface

EAGI is a slightly more advanced version of AGI, allowing the AGI script to interact with the inbound audio stream via file descriptor 3. Essentially, EAGI can be used to create applications that can tap into an inbound audio stream, analyze it, and perform tasks in accordance with that stream of data.

> The utilization of EAGI is not covered in this book.

## DeadAGI—execution on hangup

Essentially speaking, AGI requires that an active channel be available for the AGI script to run. The main idea behind this is that an AGI script is supposed to interact with the user, or make the dialplan access various aspects outside the Asterisk environment.

A question that can be asked is: "In many scenarios we would like to execute commands upon the finalization of the call, or to be more exact, upon hangup or error. How can we run an AGI script upon hangup or error?" Well, the answer is: "By means of the utilization of the DeadAGI."

DeadAGI enables the execution of an AGI script on a hung-up channel, or a channel that has not been fully established yet (in general, a non-answering channel).

> While the above behaviour is true for versions 1.0.X and 1.2.X of Asterisk, version 1.4.X generates a warning upon the execution of a DeadAGI on a channel that has just been established, even if not answered. Asterisk 1.6.X is supposed to include a facility that will enable it to decide what type of AGI operation to utilize, making the DeadAGI application obsolete.

Let's now examine how a DeadAGI script is invoked from within the Asterisk dialplan:

```
exten => h,1,DeadAGI(some_script_name.agi,param1,param2,param3)
```

The invocation is similar to that of a regular AGI script. However, DeadAGI scripts are supposed to be executed by the h extension only, or via the 'failed' extension mentioned in Chapter 2.

## FastAGI—AGI execution via a TCP socket

Technically speaking, FastAGI is different in the following context: when Asterisk executes an AGI script via FastAGI, the resources required for the AGI script to run are consumed by a completely different process, and not Asterisk. In addition, the communications that were previously based on internal STDIN/STDOUT communications are now based on a TCP socket. This means that your AGI script, now actually an AGI server, can be operated and maintained on a completely different server, enabling you to separate the application logic from the Asterisk dialplan logic.

> Bear in mind the following that if your FastAGI server has executed an internal Asterisk application (for example, playback), you will consume the resources of both the Asterisk application and the AGI execution client.

Let's now examine how a FastAGI script is invoked from within the Asterisk dialplan:

```
exten => _X.,1,AGI(agi://IP_NUMBER:PORT/some_script_name.agi)
```

Please note that passing arguments to the FastAGI servers is possible. However, it varies depending on the Asterisk version you are using.

## Asterisk 1.2.X and 1.4.X

Passing arguments to a FastAGI server from either Asterisk 1.2.X or Asterisk 1.4.X is performed by using an HTTP GET type request:

```
exten => _X.,1,AGI(agi://192.168.2.1:1048/TestAGI?exten=${EXTEN})
```

In this case, the FastAGI server is responsible for handling the various arguments, parsing them, and handling each of them correctly.

## Asterisk 1.6.X

Passing arguments to a FastAGI server from Asterisk 1.6.X is simpler and highly resembles the methodology used for a regular AGI script:

```
exten => _X.,1,AGI(agi://192.168.2.1:1048/TestAGI|${EXTEN}|{VAR2})
```

In this scenario, the arguments are available via the AGI variables named `agi_arg_1` and `agi_arg_2` respectively. The previous ones are also supported. However, if you are using Asterisk 1.6, try to use the new methodology, in order to be forward compatible.

## FastAGI frameworks

As indicated above, FastAGI is a TCP socket based system, making it a client/server environment. As with any client/server environment that is based upon an open source technology, a multitude of frameworks exist in order to make our life easier in the development of FastAGI servers. The following is a short list of frameworks, available for various platforms that do just that:

| Language | Framework | URL |
|---|---|---|
| .NET | NAsterisk | http://www.codeplex.com/nasterisk |
| ActiveX | AstOCX | http://www.pcbest.net/astocx.htm |
| Erlang | ErlAst | http://tools.assembla.com/erlast |
| Python | FATS | http://fats.burus.org/ |
|  | StarPy | http://www.vrplumber.com/programming/starpy/ |
| Java | Asterisk-Java | http://www.voip-info.org/wiki/view/Asterisk-java |
| Ruby | Adhearsion | http://docs.adhearsion.com/display/adhearison/Home |

Others exist too; however, these are the most common ones for Asterisk FastAGI development.

## AGI scripting frameworks

As with any other open source project, the number of frameworks built for the development of AGI scripts is amazing. Considering the fact that the AGI language consists of less than thirty different methods, the existence of over thirty different scripting frameworks is amazing.

The following list contains some of the more popular frameworks for AGI scripting:

| Language | Framework | URL |
| --- | --- | --- |
| PERL | Asterisk PERL Library | http://asterisk.gnuinter.net/ |
| PHP | PHPAGI | http://sourceforge.net/projects/phpagi/ |
| Python | py-Asterisk | http://py-asterisk.berlios.de/py-asterisk.php |
| C | libagiNow | http://www.open-tk.de/libagiNow/ |
| .NET | MONO-TONE | http://gundy.org/asterisk |

## The AGI application

The following is the documentation of the AGI dialplan command, as it appears in the Asterisk documentation:

### -= Info about application 'AGI' =-

```
[Synopsis]
Executes an AGI compliant application

[Description]
   [E|Dead]AGI(command|args): Executes an Asterisk Gateway Interface
compliant program on a channel. AGI allows Asterisk to launch external
programs written in any language to control a telephony channel, play
audio, read DTMF digits, etc. by communicating with the AGI protocol
on stdin and stdout.

   This channel will stop dialplan execution on hangup inside of this
application, except when using DeadAGI.  Otherwise, dialplan execution
will continue normally.
```

```
    A locally executed AGI script will receive SIGHUP on hangup from
the channel except when using DeadAGI. This can be disabled by setting
the AGISIGHUP channel variable to "no" before executing the AGI
application.
    Using 'EAGI' provides enhanced AGI, with incoming audio available
out of band on file descriptor 3
    Use the CLI command 'agi show' to list available agi commands
    This application sets the following channel variable upon
completion:
        AGISTATUS       The status of the attempt to the run the AGI
script text string, one of SUCCESS | FAILURE | HANGUP
```

Confusing? Well, for the first time you read this, it may actually be very confusing. Let's demystify AGI, shall we?

# The AGI execution flow

Once an AGI script has been invoked, a preset information flow is performed between the AGI script and Asterisk. It is imperative to understand this information flow, as the structure of your AGI script depends on this flow.

The following diagram describes the steps that occur when an AGI script is executed from within the Asterisk dialplan:

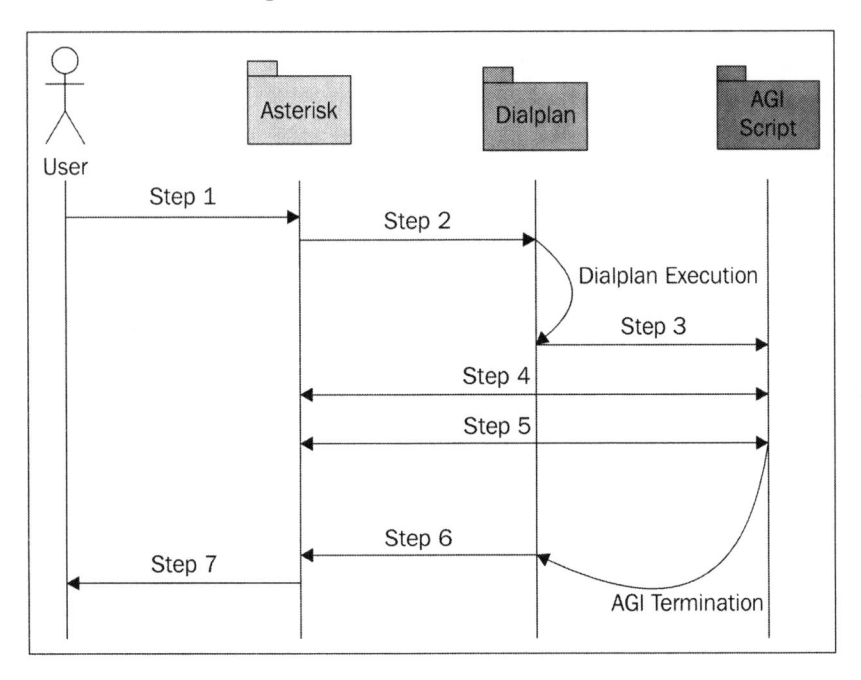

> If you are familiar with UML, the immediately preceding diagram may seem a little weird, as it doesn't follow the exact rules of the UML diagram. The diagram is meant for non-UML readers to be able to relate to the information.

As you can see, most of the interaction between Asterisk and our AGI script happens between the third and the fifth stages,. Let's examine what happens in these stages, using the following dialplan example:

```
exten => _X.,1,Answer
exten => _X.,n,Set(DID=${EXTEN})
exten => _X.,n,Set(CLID=${CALLERID(num)})
exten => _X.,n,AGI(SomeScript.php)
```

As our AGI script is being executed from the Asterisk dialplan, Asterisk will pass a preset number of variables, along with general AGI execution information to our AGI script, which requires initial processing, prior to the actual AGI script execution.

| AGI Variable | Description |
| --- | --- |
| agi_request | Name of the agi script that is being called |
| agi_channel | Channel that the call is coming from |
| agi_language | Language that is configured on the server |
| agi_type | Call type; mainly the channel type |
| agi_uniqueid | A unique identifier for this session |
| agi_callerid | Caller ID number |
| agi_calleridname | Caller ID name, where available; not supported on all channel types |
| agi_callingpres | PRI Call ID presentation variable |
| agi_callingani2 | Caller ANI2 (PRI channels), where applicable |
| agi_callington | Caller type of number (PRI channels) |
| agi_callingtns | Transit Network Selector (PRI channels) |
| agi_dnid | Dialed number identifier |
| agi_rdnis | Redirected Dial Number ID Service (RDNIS) |
| agi_context | Current context from which the AGI script was executed |
| agi_extension | Extension that was called |
| agi_priority | Current priority in the dialplan, that is, priority of the AGI script execution |
| agi_enhanced | 0.0 |
| agi_accountcode | Account code |

As your script is being executed, all the information presented in the table, will be dumped into your script execution input, before you receive any other input from Asterisk.

At the time of writing this book, the set of variables presented in the table were found to be correct. However, it is highly probable that by the time you read this book, AGI execution will include some additional variables.

> Most AGI scripts may regard the above as "noise", as most AGI scripts will obtain the information contained within these variables from an external source. When using a framework, you would notice that most frameworks simply disregard this information, and continue execution after simply skipping this portion of the execution.

Once our AGI script has finalized the information reading from Asterisk, our actual AGI script operations flow will begin, that is, our AGI script logic will begin its implementation. As we've already learned, AGI uses STDIN and STDOUT to communicate with Asterisk. In the next chapter, we shall start working with an actual AGI script. However, in the meantime knowledge of these streams is enough.

Once an AGI script has terminated its execution, it will return the control back to Asterisk for the continued execution of the Asterisk dialplan.

## The AGI methods API

The following is a complete list of AGI methods, available to the developer via the AGI interface. This list was correct at the time of writing this book, although it may change slightly by the time you read this book. It is best to update yourself via the Asterisk documentation of the AGI command, or via the `agi show` command, available from your Asterisk CLI.

```
*CLI> agi show
              answer           Answer channel
      channel status           Returns status of the connected channel
        database del           Removes database key/value
    database deltree           Removes database keytree/value
        database get           Gets database value
        database put           Adds/updates database value
                exec           Executes a given Application
            get data           Prompts for DTMF on a channel
   get full variable           Evaluates a channel expression
          get option           Stream file, prompt for DTMF, with timeout
        get variable           Gets a channel variable
```

| Command | Description |
|---|---|
| hangup | Hangup the current channel |
| noop | Does nothing |
| receive char | Receives one character from channels supporting it |
| receive text | Receives text from channels supporting it |
| record file | Records to a given file |
| say alpha | Says a given character string |
| say digits | Says a given digit string |
| say number | Says a given number |
| say phonetic | Says a given character string with phonetics |
| say date | Says a given date |
| say time | Says a given time |
| say datetime | Says a given time as specfied by the format given |
| send image | Sends images to channels supporting it |
| send text | Sends text to channels supporting it |
| set autohangup | Autohangup channel in some time |
| set callerid | Sets callerid for the current channel |
| set context | Sets channel context |
| set extension | Changes channel extension |
| set music | Enable/Disable Music on hold generator |
| set priority | Set channel dialplan priority |
| set variable | Sets a channel variable |
| stream file | Sends audio file on channel |
| control stream file | Sends audio file on channel and allows the listner to control the stream |
| tdd mode | Toggles TDD mode (for the deaf) |
| verbose | Logs a message to the asterisk verbose log |
| wait for digit | Waits for a digit to be pressed |

# The ten rules of AGI development

Developers, who are given the task of developing an AGI script for the first time, tend to superimpose their traditional development techniques over the development of AGI scripts. By far, this is the most dangerous thing that can be done, as AGI scripting and traditional programming vary immensely. The following section will list the do's and don'ts that need to be followed, so that your AGI scripts work and function properly.

# Rule #1: An AGI script should terminate as fast as possible

First-time AGI developers tend to develop their entire application within an AGI script. As you develop your entire application within an AGI script, you may gain the power of the scripting language, but will incur a cost of performance. Always make sure that the AGI scripts that you develop terminate their execution as fast as possible, returning to the dialplan as fast as possible. This concept dictates that each AGI script being run should behave quickly as an atomic unit—hence the name "Atomic AGI". We will learn the concepts of "Atomic AGI" development in Chapter 6.

# Rule #2: Blocking applications have no place in AGI

As a direct continuation to rule #1, you should never execute a blocking application from within an AGI script. Initiating a blocking application from within an AGI script will make your Asterisk environment explode slowly. Why is that? Because for every blocking application that you run from within the AGI script, you will have both your AGI script and the blocking application running for the duration of the block. Imagine that you were to initiate the Dial application from within an AGI script, and the call created would last over thirty minutes. For those thirty minutes, your AGI script is still active. This isn't much of a problem when dealing with small-scale systems. But when trying to run 50 concurrent scripts, be prepared for failure.

Blocking applications include the following: Dial, MeetMe, MusicOnHold, Playback (when dealing with long playbacks), Monitor, ChanSpy, and other applications that have an unknown execution duration.

# Rule #3: Asterisk channels are stateful—use them

An Asterisk channel, once operational, is like a big bucket of information. Channel variables can be used to carry information from your AGI script to the dialplan and back. The variables remain as part of the channel untill the channel is terminated, when memory is then freed.

Using this "bucket" enables you to carry variables and information obtained via an AGI script and then pass these to an application in the dialplan. For example, imagine that you are developing a pre-paid platform. A decision on the call timeout is taken via an AGI script. However, the actual dialling of the call is performed from the dialplan itself.

## Rule #4: AGI scripts should manipulate data—no more

Most developers tend to think of AGI scripting as a functional unit, meaning that they enclose multiple functionalities into the AGI script. While AGI is fully capable of performing telephony functionality, it is best to leave this functionality to the dialplan.

Utilize your AGI script to set and reset channel variables and communicate with out-of-band information systems. The concept of allowing out-of-band information flow into Asterisk's operational flow of channel, enables new functionality and possibilities. Not all logic should be handled by your AGI script. Sometimes, it is better to use the AGI script as a data conduit, while letting an external information system handle the data manipulation.

## Rule #5: VM based languages are bad for AGI scripting

Virtual machine based programming languages' are bad for AGI scripting. Putting aside the rules #1 and #2, imagine that your application is built using an AGI script using the Java programming language. If you are familiar with Java, you most probably know that for each program that you execute using Java, a full Java virtual machine is invoked.

While this practice may seem fairly normal for information systems, Asterisk and IVR development vary. Imagine that our system is required to handle a maximum number of 120 concurrent channels, which means that the maximum number of concurrent AGI scripts will be 120. According to this concept, our Java environment will be fully invoked for each of these 120 instances. In other words, too many resources are being used just for the VM.

If you really feel that you want to develop AGI scripts using Java, FastAGI is the way to go for you.

## Rule #6: Binary-compiled AGI is not always the answer

While evaluating rules #1, #2 and #5, we can't but reach an almost immediate conclusion that we need to have our AGI script binary compiled. While in terms of efficiency and performance, a binary compiled AGI may provide better performance, the time required to develop it may be longer. In some cases, scripting languages such as PHP, PERL, and Python may provide near-similar performance at a lesser cost.

Also, when using binary compiled AGI scripts, you are always in charge of the memory allocation and cleanup. Even the most experienced developer can commit errors while dealing with memory allocation, so binary compiled AGI need not be the solution always.

If your system truly requires the performance edge of a binary compiled AGI, we encourage you to develop a prototype using a scripting language. Once you have your prototype working, start developing your binary version.

# Rule #7: Balance your scripts with dialplan logic

While evaluating rules #1, #2 and #4, we must keep in mind that developing IVR systems with Asterisk resembles a high-wire balancing act. The fine art of balancing your dialplan with AGI scripts proves to be a powerful tool, especially when developing complex IVR systems.

Many developers tend to externalize functionality from the dialplan into AGI, while the same functionality can be achieved by writing dialplan macros or dialplan contexts. Using Asterisk's branching commands (goto, gotoif, exec, execif, gosub and gosubif) can easily remove redundant AGI code, passing the control from the AGI back to the dialplan.

> When I developed my first system, I was amazed at the sheer magnitude of the impact that rule #7 can have on a system. A system that was developed entirely with AGI, and a system achieving the same functionality using a combination of AGI and dialplan, differed by a magnitude of eight (instead of being able to sustain fifteen calls, the system sustained 120 calls), in favour of the AGI and dialplan combination. Of course, your results may vary, according to your system.

# Rule #8: Balance your scripts with web services

When evaluating rule #4, one may ask: "What is an out-of-band information system?" We shall explain now. Most Asterisk developers tend to develop their systems with the data information system—either embedded into their Asterisk server or communicating with an information system installed on the same server with the Asterisk server.

While, for small systems, this proves to be both efficient and economic, when developing a high-end system that requires scalability and redundancy, this methodology proves to be counter-productive. One of the methodologies (although many others exist) for interconnecting Asterisk with an out-of-band information system is web services. Communication to the web service is performed via AGI; the web-service protocol—you can use your favourite one.

> The choice of protocol isn't that important, as almost any protocol type used for web services would do. Be it SOAP, WSDL, XML-RPC, WDDX or any other, take your pick, and the performance and scalability should be similar in any of these.

## Rule #9: Syslog is your friend—use it

Every developer knows that using log files for debugging and monitoring purposes is a must. Be it for using a binary compiled AGI or a scripting language based AGI, make sure to utilize the logging facility. Trying to debug an AGI application from within the Asterisk console, though possible, can prove to be a tedious task. Sending log entries to a well-formatted log can save you much time and headache.

Scripting languages, such as PHP and PERL, do not offer a direct debugging facility, making the debugging of such AGI scripts even harder. Using log files as a debugging point for your AGI script will prove very useful when developing highly complex systems.

> In order to make your syslog more readable, assign a self-created unique ID to each of your calls. When writing to your log, make sure that the unique ID appears in each log entry, so that you can trace a specific session flow through Asterisk. Remember, an Asterisk channel is stateful. The unique ID will remain as part of the channel untill it is removed from the system.

## Rule #10: The Internet is for Asterisk

As bad as the following may sound, if you have a problem or an idea, remember that someone else had almost definitely come across it before you did. I don't want to discourage you, but actually, I want you to make use of the multitude of Asterisk resources available on the Internet.

The amount of information relating to Asterisk and platform development that has been accumulated by search engines is staggering. Over the course of the past two years, the amount of information available has multiplied two times (at least), making it the best source to find answers to your questions.

Asterisk user forums exist today in almost every country around the world; in some countries, there is more than one forum. These forums provide fast answers and professional guidance, allowing you to concentrate on your development, instead of concentrating on obtaining information.

> When I first started developing AGI applications (almost six years ago), information was fairly scarce. While websites like www.voip-info.org and www.asterisk.org contained most of the information, much of the experience of the other developers was not documented. Today, most of these developers write personal blogs, updated almost daily, with answers and techniques for almost any Asterisk related issue. User forums have become more and more professional, thereby making these your best choice for information.
> Other sources of information include the Asterisk IRC channel (#asterisk @ irc.freenode.net), the various Asterisk mailing lists available at the Asterisk community website, and of course the almighty Google.

# A preface to what's coming ahead

Over the course of the forthcoming chapters, we shall begin our descent into AGI development. The choice of programming language for this book is PHP, due to its popularity and ease of development. If you feel uncomfortable with PHP, we are confident that you will be able to translate the code snippets into the programming/scripting language of your choice.

Chapter 5 will deal with your first AGI script; think of it as your "Hello-World" program from "Programming 101".

Chapter 6 will introduce a PHP based AGI class library, called PHPAGI. While PHPAGI is a fairly old library, and is compatible with all the versions of Asterisk, AGI hasn't changed dramatically from one the Asterisk version to the next. By using PHPAGI and the nine rules we just saw, we shall show that even an old, slightly outdated library, can do wonders.

Chapter 7 will introduce the basic elements of a FastAGI server, again using PHP and PHPAGI.

Chapter 8 will introduce the Asterisk Manager Interface (AMI), an Asterisk proprietary CTI (Computer Telephony Integration) interface.

Chapter 9 will take you through the steps of developing a full click-2-call application, using all the concepts you've learned. Chapter 9 can be used as a basis for a large scale service, such as JaJah or RebTel.

## Summary

We have now completed our introduction to Asterisk's AGI technology. While AGI proves to be a fairly simplistic development API, the usage of AGI within your system requires you to be fully aware of your technological barriers. Be it Asterisk itself, your choice of programming/scripting language, your information systems, or the required user interaction, all these have to come into play while developing IVR systems with Asterisk and AGI.

# 5
# AGI Scripting with PHP

*Theory is when you know something, but it doesn't work. Practice is when something works, but you don't know why. Programmers combine theory and practice: Nothing works and they don't know why.* –Anonymous Developer

While much can be said about the theory of programming in general and the theory of developing with the Asterisk framework, one thing remains—any working solution is considered a good solution.

This chapter deals with your first ever AGI script, using the PHP scripting language. While the chapter deals with the most basic elements of AGI scripting and the information contained within, it won't be used as it is in the rest of the book. So take time to familiarize yourself with this chapter, especially if you intend to use a language different from PHP.

## PHP-CLI vs. PHP-CGI

Most Linux distributions include both versions of PHP when installed, especially if you are using a modern distribution such as CentOS or Mandriva. When writing AGI scripts with PHP, it is imperative that you use PHP-CLI, and not PHP-CGI.

Why is this so important? The main issue is that PHP-CLI and PHP-CGI handle their STDIN (standard input) slightly differently, which makes the reading of channel variables via PHP-CGI slightly more problematic.

# The php.ini configuration file

The PHP interpreter includes a configuration file that defines a set of defaults for the interpreter. For your scripts to work in an efficient manner, the following must be set—either via the `php.ini` file, or by your PHP script:

```
ob_implicit_flush(false);
set_time_limit(5);
error_log = filename;
error_reporting(0);
```

The above code snippet performs the following:

| Directive | Description |
| --- | --- |
| `ob_implicit_flush(false);` | Sets your PHP output buffering to `false`, in order to make sure that output from your AGI script to Asterisk is not buffered, and takes longer to execute. |
| `set_time_limit(5);` | Sets a time limit on your AGI scripts to verify that they don't extend beyond a reasonable time of execution; there is no rule of thumb relating to the actual value; it is highly dependant on your implementation. |
| | Depending on your system and applications, your maximum time limit may be set to any value; however, we suggest that you verify your scripts, and are able to work with a maximum limit of 30 seconds. |
| `error_log = filename;` | Excellent for debugging purposes; always creates a log file. |
| `error_reporting(E_NONE);` | Does not report errors to the `error_log`; changes the value to enable different logging parameters; check the PHP website for additional information about this. |

# AGI script permissions

All AGI scripts must be located in the directory `/var/lib/asterisk/agi-bin`, which is Asterisk's default directory for AGI scripts. All AGI scripts should have the execute permission, and should be owned by the user running Asterisk. If you are unfamiliar with these, consult with your system administrator for additional information.

# The structure of a PHP based AGI script

Every PHP based AGI script takes the following form:

```
#!/usr/bin/php -q
<?
    $stdin = fopen('php://stdin', 'r');
    $stdout = fopen('php://stdout', 'w');
    $stdlog = fopen('my_agi.log', 'w');

    /* Operational Code starts here */
    ..
    ..
    ..
?>
```

As indicated in the previous chapter, upon execution, Asterisk transmits a set of information to our AGI script via STDIN. Handling of that input is best performed in the following manner:

```
#!/usr/bin/php -q
<?
    $stdin = fopen('php://stdin', 'r');
    $stdout = fopen('php://stdout', 'w');
    $stdlog = fopen('my_agi.log', 'w');

    /* Handling execution input from Asterisk */

    while (!feof($stdin))
    {
        $temp = fgets($stdin);
        $temp = str_replace("\n","",$temp);
        $s = explode(":",$temp);
        $agivar[$s[0]] = trim($s[1]);
        if $temp == "")
    {
        break;
        }
    }
    /* Operational Code starts here */
    ..
    ..
    ..
?>
```

Once we have handled our inbound information from the Asterisk server, we can start our actual operational flow.

# Communication between Asterisk and AGI

As indicated in the previous chapter, the communication between Asterisk and an AGI script is performed via STDIN and STDOUT (standard output). Let's examine the following diagram:

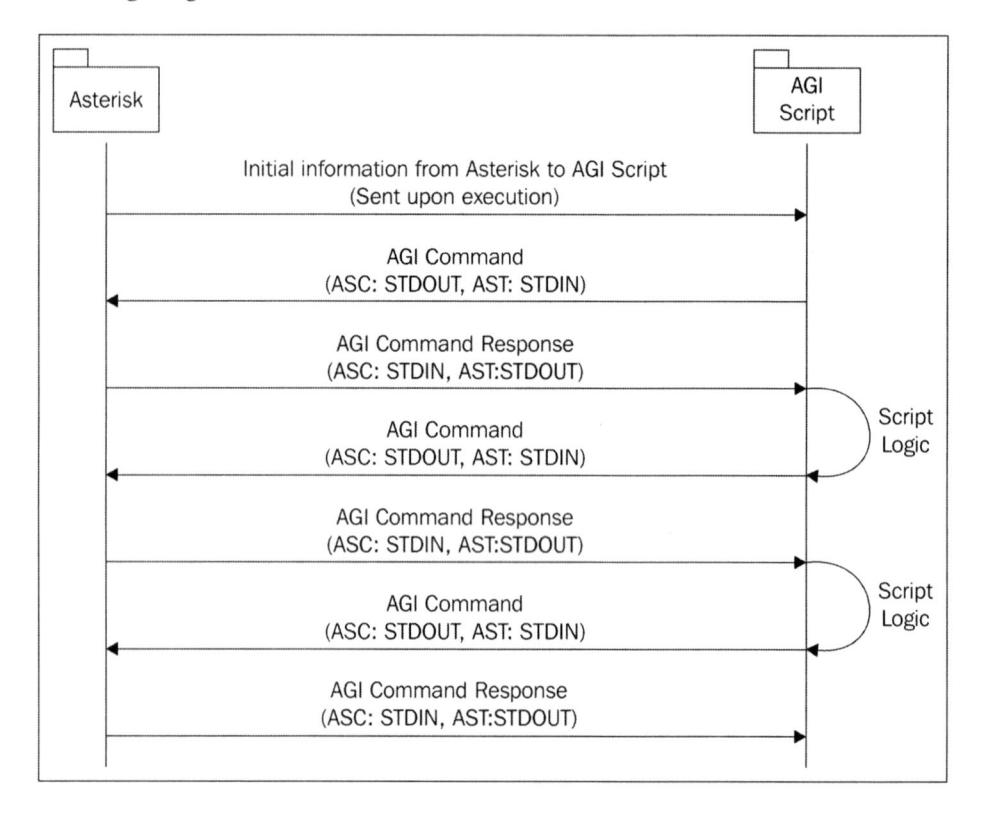

> In the above diagram, **ASC** refers to our AGI script, while **AST** refers to Asterisk itself.

As you can see from the diagram above, the entire flow is fairly simple. It is just a set of simple I/O queries and responses that are carried through the STDIN/STDOUT data streams.

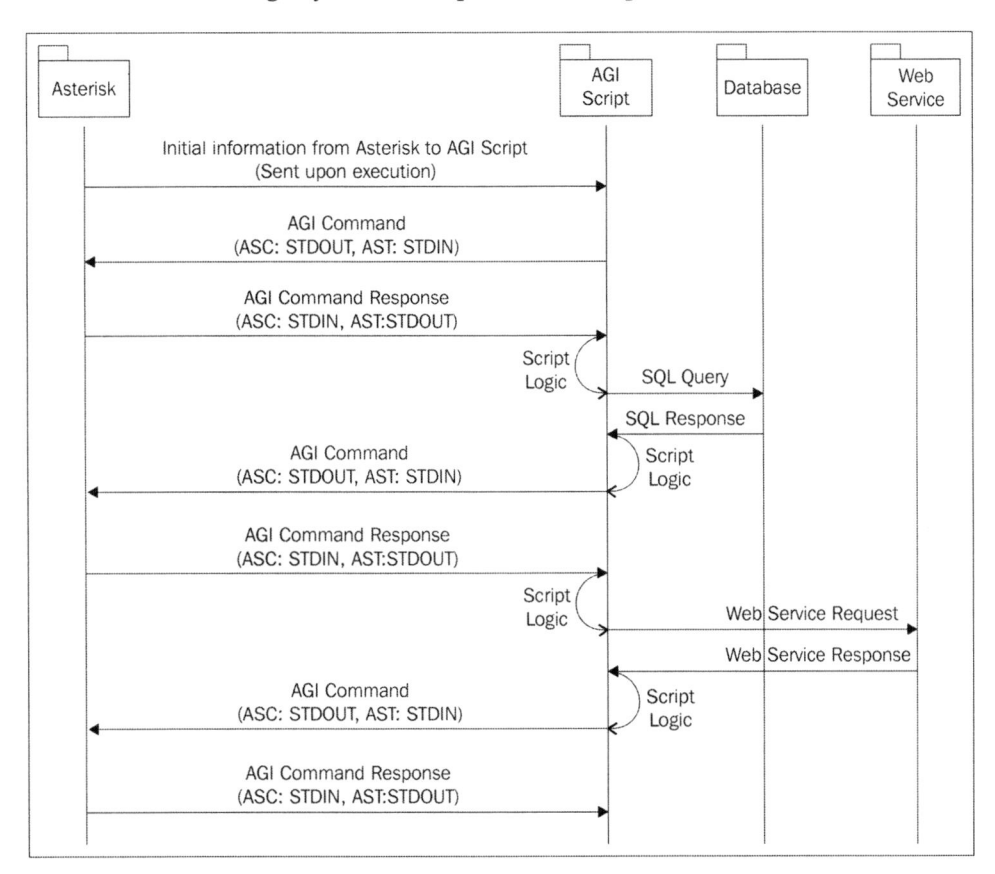

Let's now examine a slightly more complicated example:

The above figure shows an example that includes two new elements in our AGI logic—access to a database, and to information provided via a web service. For example, the immediately preceding image illustrates something that may be used as a connection between the telephony world and a dating service. This leads to an immediate conclusion that just as AGI is capable of connecting to almost any type of information source, depending solely on the implementation of the AGI script and not on Asterisk, Asterisk is capable of interfacing with almost any type of information source via out-of-band facilities.

Enough of talking! Let's write our first AGI script.

# The AGI Hello-World program

Just as with any other programming language, we shall begin our journey with a simple "Hello-World" AGI script.

# AGI Scripting with PHP

In order to make our life easier, we shall use an `astRead` function and an `astWrite` function that will help us read and write information, to and from Asterisk in a more efficient manner.

```
function astRead()
{
   global $stdin, $debug, $stdlog;
   $input = str_replace("\n", "", fgets($stdin, 4096));
   if ($debug) fputs($stdlog, "read: $input\n");
   return $input;
}

function astWrite($agiCommand)
{
   global $debug, $stdlog;
   if ($debug) fputs($stdlog, "write: $agiCommand\n");
   echo $agiCommand."\n";
}
```

The `astRead` function reads information from a global variable, indicated by the `$in` variable. The `$in` variable will simply indicate our STDIN stream. The `astWrite` function writes its `$agiCommand` directly to STDOUT, simply passing the AGI command directly to Asterisk.

Let's combine everything together:

```
#!/usr/bin/php -q
<?
   ob_implicit_flush(false);
   set_time_limit(6);

   $stdin = fopen('php://stdin', 'r');
   $stdlog = fopen('my_agi.log', 'w');

   $debug = false;

   /* Read input from Asterisk and output via $astOutput */
   function astRead()
   {
         global $stdin, $debug, $stdlog;
      $astOutput = str_replace("\n", "", fgets($stdin, 4096));
      if ($debug) fputs($stdlog, "read: $input\n");
      return $astOutput ;
   }

   /* Write AGI command to Asterisk */
   function astWrite($agiCommand)
   {
      global $debug, $stdlog;
      if ($debug) fputs($stdlog, "write: $agiCommand\n");
```

```
            echo $agiCommand."\n";
    }
    /* Handling execution input from Asterisk */

    while (!feof($stdin))
    {
            $temp = fgets($stdin);
            $temp = str_replace("\n","",$temp);
            $s = explode(":",$temp);
            $agivar[$s[0]] = trim($s[1]);
            if ($temp == "")
        {
        break;
            }
    }
    /* Operational Code starts here */
    ..
    ..
    ..
    /* Finalization of AGI script and clean-ups */
    fclose ($stdin);
    fclose ($stdlog);
    exit(0);
?>
```

The above code snippet will form our basic AGI script construct. We've now defined our stream handling functions and our Asterisk input execution handling, as we get ready to start our first AGI script.

Our first script will make use of the AGI command STREAM FILE (if you don't remember what STREAM FILE does, please refer to the previous chapter). Another command that we shall use will be SAY NUMBER.

Let's examine the following piece of code:

```
    /* Operational Code starts here */
    /* Playback the demo-congrats.gsm file from the
     * directory /var/lib/asterisk/sounds/
     */
    astWrite("STREAM FILE demo-congrats #");
    astRead();

    /* Say the number 123456 */
    astWrite("SAY NUMBER 123456 #");
    astRead();
```

*AGI Scripting with PHP*

This AGI code performs a fairly simplistic function—upon execution, it plays back the `demo-congrats.gsm` file, followed by the number `123456`. Ok, that's simple enough; so let's put everything together:

## File: helloworld.php

```
#!/usr/bin/php -q
<?
    ob_implicit_flush(false);
    set_time_limit(6);

    $stdin = fopen('php://stdin', 'r');
    $stdlog = fopen('my_agi.log', 'w');

    $debug = false;

    /* Read input from Asterisk and output via $astOutput */
    function astRead()
    {
          global $stdin, $debug, $stdlog;
       $astOutput = str_replace("\n", "", fgets($stdin, 4096));
       if ($debug) fputs($stdlog, "read: $input\n");
       return $astOutput ;
    }

    /* Write AGI command to Asterisk */
    function astWrite($agiCommand)
    {
       global $debug, $stdlog;
       if ($debug) fputs($stdlog, "write: $agiCommand\n");
       echo $agiCommand."\n";
    }

    /* Handling execution input from Asterisk */
    $agivar = array();
    while (!feof($stdin))
    {
          $temp = fgets($stdin);
          $temp = str_replace("\n","",$temp);
          $s = explode(":",$temp);
          $agivar[$s[0]] = trim($s[1]);
          if ($temp == "")
       {
          break;
          }
    }

    /* Operational Code starts here */

    /* Playback the demo-congrats.gsm file from the
```

```
     * directory /var/lib/asterisk/sounds/
     */

    astWrite("STREAM FILE demo-congrats #");
    astRead();

    /* Say the number 123456 */
    astWrite("SAY NUMBER 123456 #");
    astRead();

    /* Finalization of AGI script and clean-ups */
    fclose ($stdin);
    fclose ($stdlog);
    exit(0);

?>
```

In order to execute our AGI script, we are required to define an extension in our `extensions.conf` configuration file, and indicate the execution of our script from there. The following is an extract from the "default" context of my Asterisk server. You may insert these into any other context or extension, depending on your Asterisk server configuration:

```
exten => 999,1,Answer
exten => 999,n,Wait(0.5)
exten => 999,n,AGI(helloworld.php)
exten => 999,n,Hangup()
```

This code snippet will add a new extension named `999` to your dialplan. When this extension is dialed, your AGI script will be invoked. As your script is executed, the following can be observed on the Asterisk CLI console:

Note that as your AGI script is being executed, the only thing you will see on the CLI is the result of the AGI command, and not the actual execution of the AGI script. Also note that CLI output may vary, depending on your configuration.

## AGI debugging

Asterisk provides a means of debugging AGI Scripts as these are executed. In order to use the AGI debugger, you need to have access to Asterisk's CLI interface, and issue the following command:

```
agi debug
```

As your script is executed with debug mode enabled, your CLI output would look like this:

```
*CLI>
*CLI>
*CLI>
*CLI> agi debug
AGI Debugging Enabled
*CLI>        Executing [999@AutomaticAttendantDemo:1] Answer("SIP/3478327236-083d89c8", "") in new stack
             Executing [999@AutomaticAttendantDemo:2] Wait("SIP/3478327236-083d89c8", "0.5") in new stack
             Executing [999@AutomaticAttendantDemo:3] AGI("SIP/3478327236-083d89c8", "helloworld.php") in new stack
             Launched AGI Script /var/lib/asterisk/agi-bin/helloworld.php
AGI Tx >> agi_request: helloworld.php
AGI Tx >> agi_channel: SIP/3478327236-083d89c8
AGI Tx >> agi_language: en
AGI Tx >> agi_type: SIP
AGI Tx >> agi_uniqueid: 1215930306.1
AGI Tx >> agi_callerid: 3478327236
AGI Tx >> agi_calleridname: tvms
AGI Tx >> agi_callingpres: 0
AGI Tx >> agi_callingani2: 0
AGI Tx >> agi_callington: 0
AGI Tx >> agi_callingtns: 0
AGI Tx >> agi_dnid: 999
AGI Tx >> agi_rdnis: unknown
AGI Tx >> agi_context: AutomaticAttendantDemo
AGI Tx >> agi_extension: 999
AGI Tx >> agi_priority: 3
AGI Tx >> agi_enhanced: 0.0
AGI Tx >> agi_accountcode:
AGI Tx >>
PHP Notice:  Undefined offset:  1 in /var/lib/asterisk/agi-bin/helloworld.php on line 36
AGI Rx << STREAM FILE demo-congrats #
          Playing 'demo-congrats' (escape_digits=#) (sample_offset 0)
AGI Tx >> 200 result=35 endpos=49760
AGI Rx << SAY NUMBER 123456 #
          <SIP/3478327236-083d89c8> Playing 'digits/1' (language 'en')
          <SIP/3478327236-083d89c8> Playing 'digits/hundred' (language 'en')
          <SIP/3478327236-083d89c8> Playing 'digits/20' (language 'en')
          <SIP/3478327236-083d89c8> Playing 'digits/3' (language 'en')
          <SIP/3478327236-083d89c8> Playing 'digits/thousand' (language 'en')
          <SIP/3478327236-083d89c8> Playing 'digits/4' (language 'en')
          <SIP/3478327236-083d89c8> Playing 'digits/hundred' (language 'en')
          <SIP/3478327236-083d89c8> Playing 'digits/50' (language 'en')
          <SIP/3478327236-083d89c8> Playing 'digits/6' (language 'en')
AGI Tx >> 200 result=0
          AGI Script helloworld.php completed, returning 0
          Executing [999@AutomaticAttendantDemo:4] SoftHangup("SIP/3478327236-083d89c8", "SIP/3478327236-083d89c8") in new stack
[Jul 13 09:25:20] WARNING[10038]: app_softhangup.c:92 softhangup_exec: Soft hanging SIP/3478327236-083d89c8 up.
```

As you can see, the example in the preceding screenshot shows the full execution of the AGI script, including the initial information sent from Asterisk to the AGI script. Information traversing from Asterisk to our AGI script is prefixed with the `AGI Tx >>` marking, while information from our AGI script to Asterisk is prefixed with the `AGI Rx >>` marking. Although this may look weird, it is perfectly logical when examined from Asterisk's point-of-view.

Disabling AGI debug mode is done using the command:

`agi debug off`

> If you have enabled AGI debugging, it is imperative that you turn it off once you have completed your debug session. Debug mode outputs much information to the Asterisk console and log files, causing your Asterisk performance to be degraded.

## Summary

Congratulations! You have just written your first Asterisk AGI script. While the example that we saw previously was shown using the PHP scripting language, I am confident that you will be able to translate these examples into the programming language of your choice.

If you are an experienced programmer, we urge you to take a break from the book at this point and try to implement something different with AGI. If you are familiar with the activation of web services via CURL, try to write an AGI script to read information(like the weather) from a website and to read it out. Another option is to interface your AGI script with a database, create a username/password IVR script, and let your imagination go wild!

# 6
# PHPAGI: An AGI Class Library in PHP

*Complexity kills. It sucks the life out of developers, it makes products difficult to plan, build and test, it introduces security challenges and it causes end-user and administrator frustration. – Ray Ozzie*

When dealing with any type of development, there is nothing truer than the above statement. Complex solutions will most probably make your code difficult to maintain, and in some cases non-functional, if you are dealing with Asterisk AGI scripting.

> Over the past six years, my experience has taught me that most AGI developers who are just starting out tend to create overly complex AGI scripts. When you try to debug these, they wreak havoc on your brain and eyes. If you are already familiar with PHPAGI, the next few chapters will teach you how to utilize it better. If you are new to PHPAGI, you are at the best starting point ever.

PHPAGI had been created as a PHP-based class library, to enable faster and modular AGI development using the PHP library. PHPAGI was created in 2005, in version 1.0.X of Asterisk, making it slightly incompatible with the current version of Asterisk. However, the main incompatibility lies in how PHPAGI connects to the Asterisk manager for a specific function. However, we'll deal with that later. So in general terms, PHPAGI will provide you with a full class library for writing AGI scripts efficiently and easily.

# Obtaining PHPAGI

PHPAGI can be obtained from its community website at: `http://phpagi.sourceforge.net/`. At the time of writing this book, the released version on the PHPAGI website is 2.14. However, if you are to check the latest CVS snapshot, the latest version is 2.17.

PHPAGI is released under the **LGPL (Lesser General Public License)**, making it an ideal library for developing your AGI scripts and re-distributing them commercially—as long as your remember to include the PHPAGI license indication.

# The file structure of PHPAGI

The PHPAGI class library includes two class library files:

- `phpagi.php`: A class library for working with standard Asterisk AGI API.
- `phpagi-asmanager.php`: A class library for working with Asterisk's Manager interface via PHP. This class library is complementary to the previous one. When loaded to your AGI script, it will automatically load the previous class library as well.

In addition to the just mentioned class library files, PHPAGI includes several additional files that we'll use:

- `phpagi-fastagi.php`: This is a FastAGI bootstrap written in PHP, for turning your PHPAGI scripts into FastAGI servers.
- `phpagi.conf.example`: This is an example of the PHPAGI configuration file. This file is mandatory for your PHPAGI class library to work properly. For starters, it's enough to rename the file to `phpagi.conf`, in order to get your new scripts to work.
- `fastagi.xinetd`: This is a xinetd configuration handler for the Fast AGI bootstrap.

As we indicated earlier, all AGI scripts reside under the `/var/lib/asterisk/agi-bin` directory. It is always wise to keep all your class libraries close at hand. So, create a directory named `/var/lib/asterisk/agi-bin/include`, and copy your PHPAGI files into that directory.

# A very simple PHPAGI example

Let's assume that your PHPAGI class library files are indeed located at `/var/lib/asterisk/agi-bin/include`, and let's look at the following example:

```
1.  #!/usr/bin/php -q
2.  <?
3.    set_time_limit(30);
4.    require('include/phpagi.php');
5.    error_reporting(E_ALL);
6.
7.    $agi = new AGI();
8.
9.    $agi->answer();
10.
11.   $agi->stream_file("demo-congrats","#");
12.   do
13.   {
14.           $agi->stream_file("enter-some-digits","#");
15.           $result = $agi->get_data('beep', 3000, 20);
16.           $keys = $result['result'];
17.           $agi->stream_file("you-entered","#");
18.           $agi->say_digits($keys);
19.   } while($keys != '111');
20.   $agi->hangup();
21. ?>
```

> Don't forget to grant execution rights to your script (chmod 755 yourscript.php), so that Asterisk can execute it.

Let's examine the AGI script we've just seen:

- Lines 1-5: These provide a generic startup for our AGI script. Please note that these will be in every AGI that appears in this book.
- Line 7: This is the AGI class constructor. From this point onwards, every interaction with Asterisk will be performed via the $agi object.
- Line 9: This is our first PHPAGI directive, indicating the class library to invoke the AGI function called answer.
- Line 11: At this point, we are asking PHPAGI to play back the demo-congrats file, while allowing play back to be stopped by the # key.
- Lines 12-19: These form a loop that asks for a numeric input from the user, and then simply plays back that input to the user, using the say_digits AGI command.

Ok, that was simple enough to understand. But AGI scripts are surely more complicated than theone we saw previously, right? Of course they are! But before we continue with more complex examples, let's examine some new concepts.

# The AGI/Dialplan high-wire act

Before we continue with our script, we must learn the concept of AGI/Dialplan balancing. As you've already learned in the previous chapters, Asterisk's dialplan scripting language provides most of the facilities to enable basic IVR functionality. However, when dealing with databases and external information sources, the dialplan lacks that ability.

> While versions 1.4 and onwards of Asterisk introduced a MySQL application directly from the dialplan (part of the asterisk-addons package), its usage and results aren't easily interfaced. Thus, using external information sources via AGI is simpler and makes for a more readable dialplan.

Most developers that are just starting off with AGI tend to do the same mistake—program everything in AGI. Why is that methodology wrong? The main reason is due to the way Asterisk runs AGI scripts.

In the early versions of Asterisk, an AGI script would run in a forked Asterisk process. This meant that for every AGI script that was run, Asterisk would basically create a child process of itself, and run theAGI script within that child process. Once the AGI completed, the duplicate would be destroyed and resources will be returned.

Modern versions of Asterisk (versions 1.4 and upwards) no longer do the above. However, they perform a context-switch by running your AGI script within a small Asterisk thread. While this methodology of running an AGI script is less resource-consuming, we are still confronted with the basic problem of running AGI scripts, that is, we have a complete shell environment running for the duration of the script's work.

This behaviour immediately negates several programming languages from being used as AGI scripting candidates. For example, Java and C# maintain a full virtual machine for each execution, immediately encoring a high resource toll on your server.

> In my early days as an AGI developer, I've written several platforms with Java as my AGI scripting framework. That proved to be a bust, as I was never able to sustain more than ten virtual machines running on the server at any given time.

At this point,you would immediately say: "Well, PHP and PERL don't use a virtual machine, but the interpreter is just as bad." Right? Yes, it is true. However, the short bootstrapping of PHP and PERL makes them a more ideal choice for AGI scripting. However, it means that we need to change the way we think about AGI scripting.

# Introducing Atomic-AGI

Firstly, Atomic-AGI isn't a new form of AGI execution application from the dialplan. **Atomic-AGI** is the name I devised for a methodology for developing and deploying AGI scripts. This methodology has proved to be highly robust and reliable during the past three years.

> Atomic-AGI was devised initially during the development of an International Operator Services platform for Bezeq International in Israel. During the course of the development, the initial version was developed using a Java-based AGI framework, which proved to be problematic—both from the maintenance point of view and the performance point of view.

The term Atomic-AGI is based upon the idea that an AGI script is supposed to be as short and as simple as possible. The Atomic-AGI concept dictates the following methodologies:

- AGI scripts are used to traverse information from/to Asterisk to/from external sources.
- External sources of information are considered out-of-band information sources, and as such should be able to maintain a session for each request to the external source.
- State information should be stored within your Asterisk channel structure, unless required otherwise.
- AGI scripts never execute dialplan blocking applications (Dial, MeetMe, Voicemail, Record, and so on).
- AGI scripts should be executed from a unified execution handler, enabling a uniform methodology for handling information within the AGI script. A unified execution handler will take care of providing your AGI scripts with the proper environment they require, using various global variables, and verifying that all your AGI scripts conform to a single code style.
- AGI scripts should terminate as soon as possible, returning resources back to the Operating System/Asterisk as soon as possible.

The term **Atomic** means that we are performing particle development. Each AGI script performs a very small portion of the work, the combination between the AGI scripts and the Asterisk dialplan creates the whole.

# Atomic-AGI—a dialplan example

Let's examine the following example, showing how Atomic-AGI concepts are used within the Asterisk dialplan:

```
   [atomic-example]
1. exten => _X.,1,Answer
2. exten => _X.,n,AGI(SetSessionID.agi)
3. exten => _X.,n,AGI(agiWrapper.agi,small_agi_routing_script)
4. exten => _X.,n,Goto(atomic-${CONTEXT_FROMAGI},${EXTEN},1)
```

So, what can we see from this code snippet? On the face of it, not much, but let's examine it deeper:

- Line 1: Answers the inbound call to the PBX; nothing special there.
- Line 2: This seems like an AGI script. We shall examine the SetSessionID.agi soon. In the meantime, the script simply sets a channel variable called id_session. This variable will be used in the later sections.
- Line 3: Executes a new script called agiWrapper.agi with a parameter of small_agi_routing_script. The agiWrapper.agi script is actually a script wrapper, to be used for all of our AtomicAGI development. The result of the script is a channel variable called CONTEXT_FROMAGI.
- Line 4: Performs a Goto to the context that was set by the previous script.

As you can see, the idea here is to use the AGI scripts to basically set/unset the channel variables, and then utilize these variables within the Asterisk dialplan.

> You are probably wondering: "Why isn't SetSessionID.agi running via the agiWrapper.agi script?" Well, the main reason is that the id_session variable is used by the agiWrapper.agi script, so it has to be created before agiWrapper.agi is run. I admit that doing it this way is like shooting myself in the foot, but it's the simplest way to do it.

# SetSessionID.agi—meet your state maintainer

As noted in the previous chapters, Asterisk channels can be considered to be a stateful execution environment. This means that once a channel is active, its stored information is available for any component interaction with the channel for the entire duration of the channel's life. Interacting components may include the Asterisk dialplan, AGI script, external logic, or any other facility that may be devised by the publishing of this book.

> Bear in mind that Asterisk is an open source project. Thus, by the time this book gets published, additional information and features will be available to the developer.

Now, while the Asterisk channel is a stateful environment, our AGI scripts are not. In order to make sure that our scripts always interact with the same set of information for a specific session, we are required to generate an external session manager. `SetSessionID.agi` is exactly that session manager—a session initiator so to speak. Let's take a look at the `SetSessionID.agi` script:

```php
#!/usr/bin/php -q
<?php
   /*
    * Script:  SetSessionID.agi
    * Usage:   Preset a session ID for a channel
    * By:      Nir Simionovich, nirs@greenfieldtech.net
    * Date:    21/05/2007
    */

   $BASE_PATH="/var/lib/asterisk/agi-bin/";
   require $BASE_PATH."include/phpagi/phpagi.php";

   $sessionId = md5(uniqid());

   $agiWrapper = new AGI($BASE_PATH."include/phpagi/phpagi.conf");
   $agiWrapper->set_variable("id_session",$sessionId);
   $call_cli = $agiWrapper->get_variable("CALLERID(NUM)");

   define_syslog_variables();
   openlog("[".$sessionId."/".basename($argv[0],".php")."]",
           LOG_PID | LOG_PERROR, LOG_LOCAL2);
   syslog(LOG_INFO, "Creating session: [".$sessionId."] for CLID: 
       ".$call_cli['data']);

?>
```

Let's examine the above script section-by-section:

```php
$BASE_PATH="/var/lib/asterisk/agi-bin/";
require $BASE_PATH."include/phpagi/phpagi.php";
```

These lines include the basic PHPAGI environment in our script. Please note that I'm using the `$BASE_PATH` variables as a means to enable inclusion of additional PHP scripts in the future.

```php
$sessionId = uniqid(TRUE);

$agiWrapper = new AGI($BASE_PATH."include/phpagi/phpagi.conf");
$agiWrapper->set_variable("id_session",$sessionId);
$call_cli = $agiWrapper->get_variable("CALLERID(NUM)");
```

Using the PHP directive `uniqid`, the script will generate a unique identification key for our channel. Once the unique ID is generated, it is stored in the `$sessionId` variable. At this point, we initiate our AGI class, assigning the created object to `$agiWrapper`. From this moment onwards, any interaction with Asterisk will be performed using the `$agiWrapper` object. Our first order of business is to create a channel variable called `id_session` that will create our session ID.

```
$agiWrapper->set_variable("id_session",$sessionId);
```

Then we retrieve the inbound CALLER ID number for later use.

> Off topic: Why are we enabling `more_entropy` on the uniqid?
> The PHP function `uniqid` generates a unique identifier, based on the current time in microseconds. While it is fully possible for two machines to generate the same `uniqid` at the same time, it is fairly impossible to generate two identical unique IDs when `more_entropy=TRUE`.

```
define_syslog_variables();
openlog("[".$sessionId."/".basename($argv[0],".php")."]",
        LOG_PID | LOG_PERROR, LOG_LOCAL2);
syslog(LOG_INFO, "Creating session: [".$sessionId."] for CLID:
        ".$call_cli['data']);
```

This code snippet registers our execution to the syslog facility, indicated by `Local2`. Bear in mind that there is no direct way to debug a running AGI script based on PHP. So, your best bet would be to use proper logging.

# agiWrapper.agi—an all purpose AGI execution wrapper

Here's a problem with writing scripts: There is no unified execution and bootstrapping. What does that mean? It means that unlike normal compiled languages, most scripts tend to be somewhat chaotic, and most people developing scripts tend to do it in a fairly disorganized manner.

Another problem related to script development is the development language. As you may have noticed, this book focuses mainly on PHP. The reason it focuses on PHP is because PHP is a fairly simple and robust environment for developing Asterisk AGI scripts. However, as a friend of mine once put it: "In PHP, both a skilful developer and a newbie can develop the same application. The main difference is the maintainability of that application from that point onwards." What does that mean? It means that while you are fully capable of developing AGI scripts using vanilla PHP paradigms, the lack of proper development structures will make your AGI application difficult to maintain.

> A classic example of how poor PHP skills can develop highly complex systems is PHPNUKE. PHPNUKE is a PHP-based content management system, which has been around on the Internet for the better part of the past eight years. However, the availability and simplicity of PHP has spawned multiple, poorly written add-ons for PHPNUKE, usually resulting in serious security issues with PHPNUKE.

So, in order to make sure that our scripts always run in a unified environment, we'll need some form of bootstrapping facility for all our scripts. Our aim is to make sure that our bootstrapping script actually loads all our required include files and the channel information we may require, thereby enabling proper logging and more. So, instead of just talking about what it does, let's take a look at one of my AGI execution wrappers:

```php
<?php
/*
#
# GreenfieldTech Generic AGI Wrapper.
# Generic AGI Wrapper environment for execution of PHP based AGI scripts
# within Greenfieldtech developments.
#
# Copyright (C) 2007, Nir Simionovich, GreenfieldTech.
#
# Nir Simionovich <nirs@greenfieldtech.net>
#
# This source code is licensed under the LGPL
*/

$BASE_PATH="/var/lib/asterisk/agi-bin/";

include $BASE_PATH."../php-common/database.inc.php";
include $BASE_PATH."../php-common/config.inc.php";
require $BASE_PATH."../php-common/phpagi.php";

define_syslog_variables();

// Initiate an AGI instance
$agiWrapper     = new AGI($BASE_PATH."../php-common/phpagi.conf");
$id_session     = $agiWrapper->get_variable("id_session");

openlog("[".$id_session['data']."]/".$argv[1]."]", LOG_PID | LOG_PERROR, LOG_LOCAL2);

// Lets parse the parameters from AGI execution
$agiParameters = $argv[1];
$agiList=array();
$agiList=explode("^",$agiParameters);
syslog(LOG_INFO, "agiParameters: ".$argv[1]);

// Now that we have the AGI parameters list, lets see what we are going to execute
// Include the Platform configuration environment
include "/var/lib/asterisk/agi-bin/".$agiList[0]."/config.inc.php";

// echo "Executing ".$agiList[0]." AGI\n";
syslog(LOG_INFO, "Initiating : Platform: ".$agiList[0]." Module: ".$agiList[1]." execution");
include "/var/lib/asterisk/agi-bin/".$agiList[0]."/".$agiList[1].".inc.php";
?>
```

This script is split up into four distinct sections—the mandatory include files, initiation of the PHPAGI class, inclusion of an additional configuration file (we'll explain that in a while), and finally the inclusion of our actual operational code.

Let's examine how this code works. However as we are dealing with the inclusion of files, we first need to understand the directory structure. As you already know, all AGI scripts reside in /var/lib/asterisk/agi-bin. Over the course of time, I've found that the following directory structure helps me ensure that my scripts behave nicely:

| Directory | Purpose |
| --- | --- |
| `%var_ast%/php-common` | A directory to hold my general PHP include files including database handling files, general variables, and general configuration files. |
| `%var_ast%/agi-bin/ [PROJECT]` | In a normal situation, I would associate all my AGI scripts to a specific project; the PROJECT directory makes sure that all my script inserts are in the same place; moreover, project-specific configurations are stored in the project directory. |

Let's now examine our wrapper script:

```
$BASE_PATH="/var/lib/asterisk/agi-bin/";

include $BASE_PATH."../php-common/database.inc.php";
include $BASE_PATH."../php-common/config.inc.php";
require $BASE_PATH."../php-common/phpagi.php";
```

As you can see, the $BASE_PATH variable simply holds the physical location of the agi-bin directory. We use the $BASE_PATH variable to simply load our proper include files. In our case, they include the database.inc.php file (Sven Wagener's Database connection class), a config.inc.php file (a general configuration file) and of course, the phpagi.php file (the actual PHPAGI class file).

> Sven's database class library can be obtained from http://www.phpclasses.org/browse/author/39845.html.
> I have been using Sven's library for over three years now, and I've found it to be more than sufficient for simple MySQL usage.

```
define_syslog_variables();

// Initiate an AGI instance
$agiWrapper = new AGI($BASE_PATH."../php-common/phpagi.conf");

$id_session = $agiWrapper->get_variable("id_session");

openlog("[".$id_session['data']."/".$argv[1]."]", LOG_PID | LOG_PERROR, LOG_LOCAL2);
```

Once our include files and required classes have all been loaded, we need to initiate our environment. The PHP directive `define_syslog_variables()` initiates the PHP syslog facility, which will be used extensively in this book. The `$agiWrapper` variable is our AGI connector object. The `$agiWrapper` will provide us with the facility to communicate with Asterisk, while our AGI scripts are being executed. `$id_session` holds our independent session identifier. The `id_session` channel variable was created via the `SetSessionID.agi` script, prior to execution of our AGI script. Once we have constructed our AGI connector object and have obtained our session identifier, we open our log file for writing, so that we may send log entries from our AGI script. Note the following format:

```
[".$id_session['data']."/".$argv[1]."]
```

This format suffixes our log entries with the identified session and the value of `$argv[1]`. As indicated earlier, the variables passed from the Asterisk dialplan are passed via the `$argv` facility. So, in our case, `$argv[1]` will be the information contained in the first variable after the script name. This format will generate a log entry that looks like this:

```
Aug 16 16:03:43 centos513148 [83cf9239197797/PROJ^script1] [13380]
```

In this manner, when analyzing our log files, we can easily filter the log according to our session identifier, and then follow the execution path of our dialplan and AGI scripts.

Ok, all the include files are in place, and the syslog facility is ready. Now we need to know which project directory to access, and what project subscript to include into the execution path.

```
// Lets parse the parameters from AGI execution
$agiParameters = $argv[1];
$agiList=array();
$agiList=explode("^",$agiParameters);
syslog(LOG_INFO, "agiParameters: ".$argv[1]);
```

> Ok, I admit that the above is somewhat dirty. However, it is backward compatible with versions 1.2 and 1.0 of Asterisk. I prefer to have a backward compatible script, rather than re-write my scripts over and over and over again.

The wrapper relies on the idea that all information relating to the project and subscript are available via the `argv[1]` argument and are formatted as a ^ delimited string. For example, if our dialplan looks like this:

```
exten => _X.,n,AGI(agiWrapper.agi,PROJ^sub-script)
```

What we intend to do is activate the subscript AGI script of the project indicated by PROJ.

Once we have parsed our project and subscript, we are then ready to include our project and subscript to the AGI execution path:

```
// Now that we have the AGI parameters list, lets see what
   we are going to execute
// Include the Platform configuration environment
include "/var/lib/asterisk/agi-bin/".$agiList[0]."/config.inc.php";

// echo "Executing ".$agiList[0]." AGI\n";
syslog(LOG_INFO, "Initiating : Platform: ".$agiList[0].
   " Module: ".$agiList[1]." execution");
include "/var/lib/asterisk/agi-bin/".$agiList[0]."/".$agiList[1].
   ".inc.php";
```

Pay attention to the inclusion of the `config.inc.php` project file. This is a different configuration file, and may override the original `config.inc.php` if you may wish to do so.

Now that you are familiar with the `agiWrapper`, let's move to a slightly more complex example.

# A slightly more complex PHPAGI example

Congratulations! You've just been hired by the **Free Telephone Services Corporation** (**FTSC**) to develop a groundbreaking telephony application. FTSC would like to allow its customers to call an IVR system, enter a phone number, and make a five-minute call—free of cost.

The following flow chart has been sent to you by the marketing department (which has no idea how to write a flow chart):

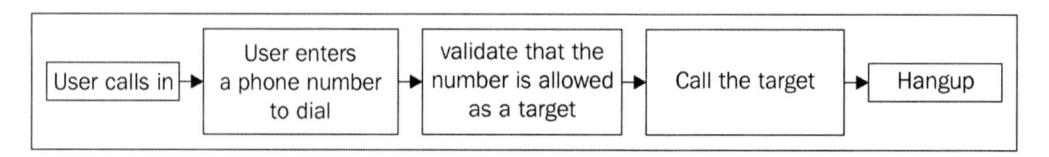

| User calls in | → | User enters a phone number to dial | → | validate that the number is allowed as a target | → | Call the target | → | Hangup |

How annoying! The marketing people of FTSC are idiots! This flow chart doesn't help me much, and is just a general description. Can't they describe it in a little more detail? Ok, let's take a deeper look and try to develop this into something more usable. So, we need to validate the number that the user wishes to connect to. So basically, we'll need to create some form of database based, country prefix authentication mechanism. So, now that we know what authentication mechanism we need, let's elaborate our flow chart.

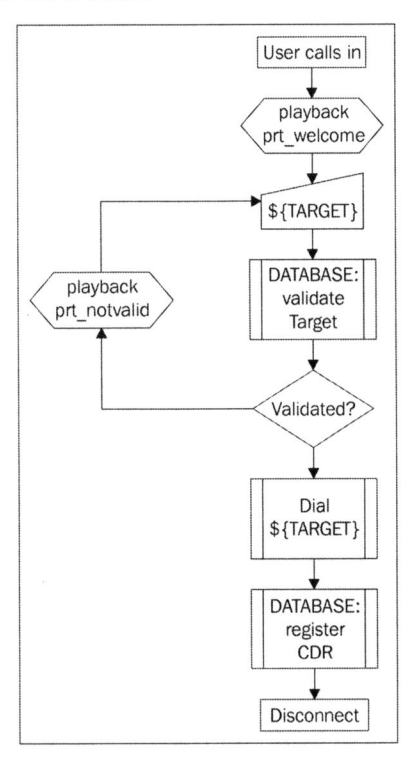

Ok, now this makes a bit more sense. To start with, let's describe our database scheme. It is clear that we need two tables—one to handle our destination prefixes and the other to handle the **CDRs (Call Detail Records)**. The following image describes our database tables:

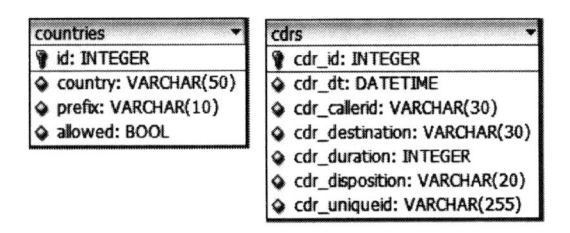

Ok, so we have a database scheme. Let's get down with some dialplan programming:

```
   [ftsc-callthrough]
1. exten => _X.,1,Answer
2. exten => _X.,n,AGI(SetSessionID.agi)
3. exten => _X.,n,Playback(prt_welcome)
4. exten => _X.,n(ReadTarget),Read(TARGET,"prt_target",,,5,5)
5. exten => _X.,n,AGI(agiWrapper.agi,FTSC^db_validate_target)
6. exten => _X.,n,GotoIf($[${VALID} = 0]?ReadTarget)
7. exten => _X.,n,Dial(Zap/g1/${TARGET},120,L(300000,60000,30000))
8. exten => _X.,n,Softhangup(${CHANNEL})

9. exten => h,1,DeadAGI(agiWrapper.agi,FTSC^db_register_cdr)
```

Ok, let's review our dialplan:

- Line 1: Answer the call.
- Line 2: Preset a session variable, indicating our session for the rest of the execution path. We've already discussed this script before.
- Line 3: Play back the welcome message.
- Lines 4-6: Read a DTMF sequence from the user, validate the target, and proceed if possible.
- Line 7: Dial the target number. We've defined the dialing timeout as `120` seconds, allowing the remote target to ring for no more than `120` seconds. In addition, the `L` parameter indicates a time limitation on the phone. We've defined a maximum call duration of `300000`mSec (300 seconds), with an alert at `60000`mSec (60 seconds) prior to the automatic termination of the call, repeated every `30000`mSec (30 seconds) untill the call is hung up by the Asterisk server.
- Line 8: Hang up the call when the call is completed. Using the `Softhangup` application enables us to hang up the call, and, when required, also continue the execution of the dialplan from that point onwards. This is very useful for pre-paid systems and timed calls scenarios.
- Line 9: Execute CDR handling once the call is completed. As you can see, we've created two new AGI script modules—`db_validate_target` and `db_register_cdr`.

> An important factor when writing AGI scripts is the naming convention of your modules. For example, you may have notice that I prefixed my modules with the abbreviation `db_`, indicating that this module deals with database access. As redundant as this may seem to you, following a preset naming convention will help you keep your script modules under control.

# db_validate_target.inc.php

The purpose of the `db_validate_target.inc.php` script module is to connect to our database, issue a SQL query to validate the target number, and then return a channel variable called VALID to the dialplan, indicating whether the validation was successful or not.

> The following section makes use of SQL queries. If you are unfamiliar with the SQL language (using the MySQL SQL engine), please refer to an SQL training manual or an online MySQL tutorial.
> A nice SQL primer on using MySQL is available at
> http://www.lsbu.ac.uk/ict/authoring/mysql/startup.shtml

The following is our script code:

```
<?
  $VALID_FLAG = 0; // Call is not valid at this point yet

  // Get the session ID information
  $session_id_raw = $agiWrapper->get_variable("id_session");
  $session_id     = $session_id_raw['data'];

  // Connect to the database - exit if error
  $db = new database(
          "mysql",
          "localhost",
          "FTSC",
          "ftscuser",
          "ftscpass");

  if (!$db) {
    syslog(LOG_INFO,"Connection to database failed");
    syslog(LOG_INFO,"SQL Error: ".mysql_error());
    exit(99);
  }

  // Get the target input from Asterisk
  $target_raw = $agiWrapper->get_variable("TARGET");
  $target     = $target_raw['data'];


  // Check the target with the countries tables
  $query = "select * from countries where '"
          .$target."' like CONCAT(prefix,'%') "
```

```
              ."and allowed=1";

   if(!$db->query($query)) {
     syslog(LOG_INFO,"MySQL query failed");
     syslog(LOG_INFO,"SQL Error: ".mysql_error());
     exit(98);
   }

   if ($db->count_rows) {
     $VALID_FLAG = 1; // Cal is valid
   }

   $agiWrapper->set_variable("VALID",1);
   $db->disconnect();
?>
```

We won't dwell into the script's inner workings. However, we would dwell into a particular section—the retrieval and assignment of variables to and from the dialplan.

As you can see, I'm using a two-stage retrieval method:

```
// Get the target input from Asterisk
$target_raw = $agiWrapper->get_variable("TARGET");
$target     = $target_raw['data'];
```

The `get_variable` method of PHPAGI returns an array. The array essentially contains the three parameters returned from Asterisk by using the AGI command `get_variable`. These include result, data, and code. As the DTMF is captured via the "Read" application, the data captured by the TARGET variable is the dialplan that is retrieved via the `get_variable` method, while the data itself is stored in the `'data'` key of the result.

> While AGI is fully capable of receiving data via the `get_data` method, this imposes an interesting issue. As long as the `get_data` method is active, our AGI script is active, which means that we are running the PHP interpreter for something that can be accomplished by the dialplan. Remember, the fine balance between AGI and the dialplan. Sometimes, using the dialplan for simple tasks is much faster and more reliable.

## db_register_cdr.inc.php

The purpose of the `db_register_cdr.inc.php` script module is to record the information of our call to our CDR database. CDR databases are used primarily for call logging and billing purposes. As you've probably noticed from the dialplan, the execution of this module is performed via the DeadAGI application, as this module needs to be executed once our call has completely terminated.

> While we've showed you the previous script, we'll let you write this specific script on your own, as a small exercise to write an AGI script using what you've learned so far.

## AGI Scripts in popular Asterisk applications

As the Asterisk community grew, so did the number of applications available for it. Asterisk applications these days range from management interfaces, IVR systems, pre-paid systems, micro payment systems, and content delivery platforms.

We shall take a look at two of the most common applications for Asterisk—a management GUI and a pre-paid calling card platform. We'll specifically take a look at FreePBX™ and A2Billing™.

## FreePBX™—the most popular Asterisk management GUI

FreePBX™ is the de-facto standard these days for an Asterisk management GUI. Being adopted by almost all of the automatic Asterisk PBX installers (TrixBox, Elastix, PBX-in-a-flash), it is currently the most complete implementation of an Asterisk-based office PBX system.

FreePBX™ makes use of a few AGI scripts, but we'll focus on only one: `dialparties.agi`.

> If you've read my previous book on *AsteriskNOW*, you must have noticed that Digium has its own Asterisk management GUI, called AsteriskGUI. As of version 1.5 of AsteriskNOW, the Asterisk GUI in *AsteriskNOW* has been replaced by FreePBX.

The `dialparties.agi` script uses the PHPAGI class library, so you should be able to go about and read it fully. The purpose of this script is to intercept calls as they traverse the PBX system, analyze their origin and target, and decide how to route the calls according to the configuration of FreePBX.

While `dialparties.agi` directly answers the "Atomic-AGI" concept, the FreePBX™ project is a spin-off from the Asterisk Management Portal project. This automatically resulted in a multitude of developers contributing code, some of whom were a bit messier than the others.

FreePBX™ makes use of a few other scripts, written by different people. If you were to analyze these scripts, you would easily notice that these scripts are completely different. That means that each script needs to be handled differently. Thus, a developer wishing to get into the FreePBX™ project would be required to study three different coding styles. Experienced developers would argue: "A good developer should be able to find heads and tails, regardless of the coding style!" Well, that is true. But why make life so complicated? If all these scripts use a single bootstrap script, and utilize the same object abstraction, it would make life so much easier for other developers to contribute.

The FreePBX™ project is available at `http://www.freepbx.org`.

## A2Billing™—a pre-paid calling card system

A2Billing™ (a.k.a. Asterisk2Billing) is an Asterisk-based pre-paid/post-paid calling cards and ITSP solution, capable of rendering services to thousands of users with up to 240 concurrent connections. The limit isn't hard coded and depends upon your hardware. It's simply a number that has been measured by various sources.

Currently, A2Billing is being used in a multitude of installations across the world, specifically operating within the calling-card market and the call-shops market.

Unlike FreePBX™, A2Billing™ uses a single AGI script to do all its magic. A short examination of the installation instructions shows that the AGI activation is as follows:

```
[a2billing]
; CallingCard application
exten => _X.,1,Answer
exten => _X.,2,Wait,2
exten => _X.,3,DeadAGI,a2billing.php
exten => _X.,4,Wait,2
exten => _X.,5,Hangup
```

> The methodology of activating an AGI using the DeadAGI application after answering the call is wrong. While it was working just fine with Asterisk 1.2.X, in Asterisk 1.4.X, it started generating warnings. In Asterisk 1.6.X, it will simply turn the execution from DeadAGI to AGI automatically, making the entire A2Billing application perform incorrect billing.

For each inbound call into the A2Billing application, the AGI script is invoked (a2billing.php). However, it means that for the entire duration of the call, the AGI script is alive and kicking, which exactly is the opposite of the Atomic-AGI concept.

The A2Billing™ project is available at http://www.a2billing.org.

# Summary

Like any other development technology, development of AGI with PHPAGI requires a certain level of finesse. Unlike traditional methodologies of development, encapsulating your entire application logic into your AGI script can be counterproductive.

If you are familiar with web technologies, try and think of developing AGI scripting using Atomic AGI concepts as an Asterisk **MVC (Model View Controller)** structure, using the PHP language. Asterisk provides our "View" layer the AGI Asterisk application, the agiWrapper script provides the "Controller", while our script modules provide the "Models".

At the end of Chapter 5, we'd asked you to write a slightly more advanced script, using a combination of CURL. Try to redevelop your script, using the concepts you've learned in this chapter.

# 7
# FastAGI: AGI as a TCP Server

*The first 90% of the code accounts for the first 90% of the development time.*
*The remaining 10% of the code accounts for the other 90% of the development time.*
–Tom Cargill

As we discussed in the previous chapters, one of the major pit-falls of AGI scripting is the methodology with which Asterisk executes AGI scripts. The nature of loading the entire script environment, whenever an AGI script is invoked, poses an interesting problem. In order to understand the problem better, let's imagine the following dialplan example:

```
[callingcard-platform]
; CallingCard application
exten => _X.,1,Answer
exten => _X.,n,AGI(callingcard.sh)
exten => _X.,n,Hangup
```

Now, let's imagine that the `callingcard.sh` shell script executes an AGI application, developed using a Java framework. The immediate result will be that for each invocation of the AGI script, we will automatically pay the overhead of a full virtual machine running in memory.

While one or two will not impose a serious load on our server, having ten or fifteen concurrent virtual machines running is a big no-no. Now, imagine that we have the ability to completely separate the AGI logic from our Asterisk server. FastAGI provides exactly this facility!

FastAGI provides a facility whereby Asterisk communicates with your AGI script via a TCP socket, instead of via the standard STDIN/STDOUT interface. FastAGI enables the developer with a means to spread the load of the application across several servers, enabling the Asterisk server to reach its top performance, because the server resources are not used for running external logic, apart from Asterisk.

The previous dialplan extract will look like this using FastAGI:

```
[callingcard-platform]
; CallingCard application
exten => _X.,1,Answer
exten => _X.,n,AGI(agi://192.168.0.1)
exten => _X.,n,Hangup
```

By default, Asterisk will connect to the FastAGI server via the TCP port 4573. However, that can be changed according to your requirements. Consider the following dialplan extract:

```
[callingcard-platform]
; CallingCard application
exten => _X.,1,Answer
exten => _X.,n,AGI(agi://192.168.0.1:6060)
exten => _X.,n,Hangup
```

Most FastAGI servers tend to implement a single application flow. However, there may be times where you may want to implement multiple AGI flows, using a single FastAGI server. In order to do that, FastAGI provides a facility to invoke a specific network location.

```
[callingcard-platform]
; CallingCard application
exten => _X.,1,Answer
exten => _X.,n,AGI(agi://192.168.0.1:6060/callingcard)
exten => _X.,n,Hangup
```

The above code snippet will connect to the FastAGI server located at 192.168.0.1 on port 6060, and will execute the AGI script indicated by the name callingcard.

## FastAGI argument handling

Similar to AGI, FastAGI provides the ability to pass variables directly from the dialplan to the FastAGI server. However, when doing so, we must pay attention to the version of Asterisk that we are using, as variations exist between the different branches of the Asterisk project.

## Asterisk 1.2.X and 1.4.X

Versions 1.2.X and 1.4.X of Asterisk handle argument passing to FastAGI server by using an HTTP GET format. Consider the following:

```
[callingcard-platform]
; CallingCard application
exten => _X.,1,Answer
exten => _X.,n,AGI(agi://192.168.0.1/callingcard&exten=${EXTEN}&c=12)
exten => _X.,n,Hangup
```

It is the responsibility of your FastAGI server to parse the information from the request, and pass the arguments to your application accordingly. Asterisk 1.2.X and 1.4.X do not provide a standard facility for passing arguments to a FastAGI server.

## Asterisk 1.6.X

Asterisk 1.6.X introduced a means of passing arguments to FastAGI servers. Consider the following:

```
[callingcard-platform]
; CallingCard application
exten => _X.,1,Answer
exten => _X.,n,AGI(agi://192.168.0.1/cc,${EXTEN},12,${CALLERID(num)})
exten => _X.,n,Hangup
```

The above example creates three arguments that are passed to our FastAGI server. As the AGI script is executed on the remote machine, the AGI information will contain the following:

```
agi_network: yes
agi_network_script: /cc
agi_arg_1: 972732557799
agi_arg_2: 12
agi_arg_3: 972546981111
```

Bear in mind that Asterisk 1.6.X still supports the previous methodology described. However, future versions may not.

## FastAGI error handling

Error handling of FastAGI is dramatically different between the different Asterisk versions.

## Asterisk 1.2.X

Asterisk 1.2.X has a fairly limited capability of handling errors encountered in the execution of a FastAGI remote script. Actually, the handling is so limited that if, for some reason, a FastAGI script fails during execution, Asterisk will simply disconnect the call.

> A patch was made available for Asterisk 1.2.X to fix the above behavior. However, as Asterisk 1.2.X is no longer supported by Digium and community, we shall not dwell on this.

## Asterisk 1.4.X and 1.6.X

Asterisk 1.4.X introduced a new methodology, similar to the one used by the normal AGI application. Upon completion of the script—be it successful or not—Asterisk will set the AGISTATUS channel variable with any one of the following values: SUCCESS, FAILURE, or HANGUP.

- SUCCESS: Indicates that the FastAGI server has completed its operation normally
- FAILURE: Indicates that the FastAGI server has terminated with an error, and should be handled accordingly
- HANGUP: Indicates that the call that invoked the AGI script has hung up the call, while the FastAGI server continues to execute the script

This methodology enables the developer to verify the results of the FastAGI server as it returns control back to Asterisk, thereby allowing the branching of the dialplan in accordance with the FastAGI server's response.

## FastAGI with PHPAGI and xinetd

If you are an experienced PHP developer, the term "Network Server" and PHP doesn't mix all that well in your mind, while a PHP-based "Network Client" seems just fine. The idea of a "Network Server", usually associated with the ability to run in multi-threaded mode, seems like an oxymoron.

However, as much as the connection between PHP and a TCP Network Server appears to be unnatural (or in some cases, downright crazy), PHPAGI includes a facility to turn your normal AGI scripts into FastAGI servers, using a FastAGI bootstrap and using the xinetd nework service.

# Introducing xintetd—the Internet services daemon

Xinetd is the successor of the inetd super-server daemon. Technically speaking, almost any modern UNIX operating system will have either an inetd or an xinetd daemon (xinetd is more secure than inetd)

The term "Super-Server" is derived from inetd's multiple port binding behavior. The super-server will "listen" on a multiple, designated Internet service ports, such as POP3, FTP, and telnet. Once a connection is made to one of the "listening" ports, the Super-Server will activate the related server binary that is associated with that specific port.

In the past, most network services were operated via the inetd super-server. As modern operating system design has evolved and with the introduction of simpler multi-threading techniques, the use of super-server has slowly diminished. However, it is still available for use, and in some cases, allows for greater granularity in security for compatible server binaries.

One of the added values of using inetd/xinetd is the fact that your server binary no longer needs to care for network-related tasks. The super-server communicates with your server binary via the STDIN/STDOUT/STDERR streams, thus allowing almost any program to become a network server.

# Configuring xinetd for FastAGI and PHPAGI

Now let's take a look at how to configure xinetd for FastAGI and PHPAGI

> For more information about the xinetd server, please refer to the xinetd community website, located at http://www.xinetd.org/.

As indicated previously, in order to turn our AGI script into a FastAGI server, we must first configure xinetd. The following is an example of what the xinetd configuration may look like:

```
# default: off
# description: fastagi is a remote AGI interface
service fastagi
{
        socket_type    = stream
        user           = root
        group          = nobody
        server         = /var/lib/asterisk/agi-bin/fastagiWrapper.php
        wait           = no
```

```
            protocol     = tcp
            bind         = 127.0.0.1
            port         = 4573
            disable      = no
}
```

The `socket_type` indicates what type of service is associated with this specific configuration. In our case, the keyword `stream` indicates that we are dealing with a stream-based service.

The `user` indicates which user ID is to be used for running the related server executable. If you require a different user to be used, you may change this setting. However, make sure that your settings allow for proper usage.

The `group` indicates which group ID is to be used for running the related server executable. If you require a different user to be used, you may change this setting. However, make sure that your settings allow for proper usage.

The `server` indicates the server executable to be executed upon receiving a connection to the designated bound IP number and port.

The `wait` determines if the service is single-threaded or multi-threaded, and who accepts the connection—the xinetd or the server program. If its value is `yes`, the service is single-threaded, meaning that xinetd will start the server, and will stop handling requests for the service until the server dies, while the server software will accept the connection. If the attribute value is `no`, the service is multi-threaded, and xinetd will keep handling new service requests and will accept the connection.

The `protocol` indicates what type of protocol we are using—TCP or UDP.

The `bind` and `port` settings indicate which IP number and PORT number our server is bound to.

The `disable` directive indicates whether our server will be available on the network or not.

As you may see from the above example, the server executable is set to `/var/lib/asterisk/agi-bin/fastagiWrapper.php`. The `fastagiWrapper.php` script is actually a bootstrapping facility, which will enable us to activate the proper AGI script via our newly-created xinetd server.

Once we have configured our xinetd super-server, we need to notify your Linux server of the new TCP service. In order to do this, add the following line to your `/etc/services` file:

```
      fastagi           4573/tcp                # Asterisk FastAGI Server
```

The first parameter indicates the name of the new service to be rendered by xinetd. The second parameter indicates the port number and the type of IP protocol to listen to (UDP or TCP).

Once you have finished your configuration, you may run the following command:

```
service xinetd restart
```

> The "service" command is mainly used with distributions such as FedoraCore, RedHat, CentOS, and the likes. If you're using a Debian distribution, or any other distribution, you may need to use a different script. Consult your distribution documentation for additional information.

If everything has been performed correctly, using the netstat -apn | less command should emit an output similar to the following:

```
Active Internet connections (servers and established)
Proto Recv-Q Send-Q Local Address           Foreign Address
State       PID/Program name
tcp        0      0 10.10.220.202:3306      0.0.0.0:*
LISTEN      2546/mysqld
tcp        0      0 0.0.0.0:5038            0.0.0.0:*
LISTEN      2771/asterisk
tcp        0      0 127.0.0.1:4573          0.0.0.0:*
LISTEN      9807/xinetd
tcp        0      0 10.10.220.202:44728     10.10.220.204:3306
ESTABLISHED 9670/php
tcp        0      0 10.10.220.202:43243     10.10.220.204:3306
ESTABLISHED 2771/asterisk
tcp        0      0 127.0.0.1:32963         127.0.0.1:4573
ESTABLISHED 2771/asterisk
tcp        0      0 127.0.0.1:32947         127.0.0.1:4573
ESTABLISHED 2771/asterisk
```

Note the following line:

```
tcp        0      0 127.0.0.1:4573          0.0.0.0:*
LISTEN      9807/xinetd
```

Our xinetd is bound to TCP port 4573, as we expect it to activate our AGI script via that port.

# Configuring PHPAGI for FastAGI

Before we start handling the actual FastAGI bootstrap, we must first configure the FastAGI environment of our PHPAGI class. By editing the `phpagi.conf` file, verify that the following code appears in it:

```
[fastagi]
setuid=true;    drop privileges to owner of script
basedir=/var/lib/asterisk/agi-bin/;    path to script folder
```

These settings will be used by our FastAGI bootstrap script.

# The fastagiWrapper.php bootstrap

The following code is based on the code available with the PHPAGI distribution:

```php
#!/usr/bin/php-cgi -q
<?php

    $BASE_PATH="/var/lib/asterisk/agi-bin/";

    include $BASE_PATH."../php-common/database.inc.php";
    include $BASE_PATH."../php-common/config.inc.php";
    require $BASE_PATH."../php-common/phpagi.php";

    define_syslog_variables();

    // Initiate an array for local channel variable keeping
    $agiVariables = array();

    // Initiate an AGI instance
    $agiWrapper    = new AGI($BASE_PATH."../php-common/phpagi.conf");

    if(!isset($agiWrapper->config['fastagi']['basedir']))
        $fastagi->config['fastagi']['basedir'] = dirname(__FILE__);

    $script = $fastagi->config['fastagi']['basedir'] .
    DIRECTORY_SEPARATOR . $agiWrapper->request['agi_network_script'];

    $id_session = $agiWrapper->get_variable("id_session");
    openlog("[".$id_session['data']."/".$agiWrapper->request
      ['agi_network_script']."]", LOG_PID | LOG_PERROR, LOG_LOCAL2);

    // make sure the script executable exists, or bail out
    if(!file_exists($script)) {
        syslog(LOG_INFO,"$script does not exist");
        exit;
```

```
        }

        // drop privileges
        if(isset($agiWrapper->config['fastagi']['setuid']) &&
            $agiWrapper->config['fastagi']['setuid']) {
                $owner = fileowner($script);
                $group = filegroup($script);
                if(!posix_setgid($group) || !posix_setegid($group)
                    || !posix_setuid($owner) || !posix_seteuid($owner)) {
                        syslog(LOG_INFO,"$script failed to lower
                        priviliges");
                        exit;
                }
        }

        // make sure script is still readable
        if(!is_readable($script)) {
                syslog(LOG_INFO,"$script is no longer readable");
                exit;
        }

        require_once($script);
?>
```

While the script we just saw is fairly similar to the one we've used as our PHPAGI wrapper, it is slightly different. Let's examine the main differences:

```
    if(!isset($agiWrapper->config['fastagi']['basedir']))
        $fastagi->config['fastagi']['basedir'] = dirname(__FILE__);

$script = $fastagi->config['fastagi']['basedir'] .
    DIRECTORY_SEPARATOR . $agiWrapper->request['agi_network_script'];
```

The above snippet of code checks the PHPAGI configuration and extracts the FastAGI basedir definition. As you may have noticed before, we set our FastAGI basedir to /var/lib/asterisk/agi-bin. Once we have established the location of the FastAGI basedir, we construct the execution path of our FastAGI script, indicated by the agi_network_script variable (as indicated above).

For example, let's imagine that our script is invoked using the following diaplan directive:

```
exten => _X.,n,AGI(agi://192.168.0.1:6060/callingcard)
```

## FastAGI: AGI as a TCP Server

So, our `$script` variable will now contain the following:

```
$script = "/var/lib/asterisk/agi-bin/callingcard";
```

So, we've established where to read our AGI script executable from. Let's continue.

```
// drop privileges
if(isset($agiWrapper->config['fastagi']['setuid'])
    && $agiWrapper->config['fastagi']['setuid']) {
    $owner = fileowner($script);
    $group = filegroup($script);
    if(!posix_setgid($group) || !posix_setegid($group)
    || !posix_setuid($owner) || !posix_seteuid($owner)) {
        syslog(LOG_INFO,"$script failed to lower
        priviliges");
        exit;
    }
}
```

The above code snippet sets the execution privileges of our AGI script to those of the script owner. The reason we are doing this is because the xinetd super server is run using the `root` privilege, thus introducing a massive security hole.

> Unlike running an AGI script on its own, using a FastAGI introduces an interesting security concern. Although Asterisk will execute the connection to the FastAGI server using Asterisk's privileges, the FastAGI server may be run with a completely different privilege set. This is especially true if your FastAGI server is running on a completely different server. Remember, if you run your FastAGI servers as root, you may expose your system to security issues. So, never run your FastAGI servers as root (unless you really have to)!

As a rule of thumb, create an unprivileged user to run your AGI scripts, thereby locking your scripts to run in a closed environment—a good practice to follow.

```
// make sure script is still readable
if(!is_readable($script)) {
    syslog(LOG_INFO,"$script is no longer readable");
    exit;
}

require_once($script);
```

Once we have changed the privileges of the execution, we must verify that our script is readable, prior to the execution of the script. This will verify that our current script privileges and the script executable are compatible, and that the script file can be read by our bootstrap.

Once this is achieved, the next step is to perform a `require_once` to our AGI script file, and our FastAGI is now ready to run.

## Performance consideration

As indicated before, PHP isn't an all round multi-threading environment! In order to make the above statement clean, examine the following output of the `ps auxf` command:

```
asterisk       9817  0.0  0.1 192280 11604 ?        Ss   13:32   0:00
\_ /usr/bin/php-cgi -q /var/lib/asterisk/agi-bin/fastagi.php
asterisk       9852  0.0  0.1 192280 11604 ?        Ss   13:33   0:00
\_ /usr/bin/php-cgi -q /var/lib/asterisk/agi-bin/fastagi.php
asterisk       9944  0.9  0.1 192288 11608 ?        Ss   13:40   0:00
\_ /usr/bin/php-cgi -q /var/lib/asterisk/agi-bin/fastagi.php
```

This is an output from a system that runs three sessions of a FastAGI server, based on PHP and PHPAGI. As you can see, there is no difference between running three instances of a simple AGI script and running three instances of the same script as a FastAGI instance.

## FastAGI with PHPAGI and Google

As we've already learned, PHP isn't the most natural approach for writing FastAGI servers. However, that doesn't have to be the default. Although PHP provides facilities for creating non-blocking sockets, writing a multi-client TCP daemon using PHP isn't a simple task. Thankfully, the good people at Google had released an LGPL library for creating non-blocking, asynchronous, high-performance socket routines, based on PHP. Initially, the project was created as a base for an IRC web application.

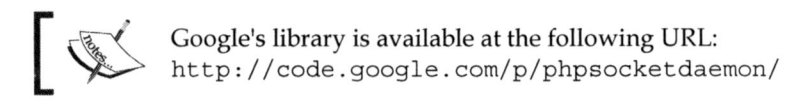

> Google's library is available at the following URL:
> `http://code.google.com/p/phpsocketdaemon/`

Google's library is fairly simplistic. However, it may assist a developer with the development of high-performance FastAGI scripts with PHP. The library is fully objectified. So, if you're not familiar with PHP-OO, the following code could seem really wierd. The following code creates a simple HTTP socket server, using the Google library:

## httpd.php:

```php
#!/usr/bin/php -Cq
<?
/*
phpSocketDaemon 1.0
Copyright (C) 2006 Chris Chabot <chabotc@xs4all.nl>
See http://www.chabotc.nl/ for more information

This library is free software; you can redistribute it and/or
modify it under the terms of the GNU Lesser General Public
License as published by the Free Software Foundation; either
version 2.1 of the License, or (at your option) any later version.

This library is distributed in the hope that it will be useful,
but WITHOUT ANY WARRANTY; without even the implied warranty of
MERCHANTABILITY or FITNESS FOR A PARTICULAR PURPOSE.  See the GNU
Lesser General Public License for more details.

You should have received a copy of the GNU Lesser General Public
License along with this library; if not, write to the Free Software
Foundation, Inc., 51 Franklin Street, Fifth Floor, Boston, MA
02110-1301  USA
*/

ini_set('mbstring.func_overload', '0');
ini_set('output_handler', '');
error_reporting(E_ALL | E_STRICT);
@ob_end_flush();
set_time_limit(0);
include("socket.php");
include("httpServer.php");

$daemon = new socketDaemon();
$server = $daemon->create_server('httpdServer', 'httpdServerClient', 0, 2001);
$daemon->process();
```

This code creates a socket server that is listening at TCP port 2001. The method called `create_server` actually receives the name of a server object, which describes the methods that the server implements.

The `httpdServer` object indicated in the code, is included from the `httpServer.php` file that is included at the beginning of the script.

## httpServer.php:

```
<?
/*
phpSocketDaemon 1.0 - httpd server demo implementation
Copyright (C) 2006 Chris Chabot <chabotc@xs4all.nl>
See http://www.chabotc.nl/ for more information

This library is free software; you can redistribute it and/or
modify it under the terms of the GNU Lesser General Public
License as published by the Free Software Foundation; either
version 2.1 of the License, or (at your option) any later version.

This library is distributed in the hope that it will be useful,
but WITHOUT ANY WARRANTY; without even the implied warranty of
MERCHANTABILITY or FITNESS FOR A PARTICULAR PURPOSE.  See the GNU
Lesser General Public License for more details.

You should have received a copy of the GNU Lesser General Public
License along with this library; if not, write to the Free Software
Foundation, Inc., 51 Franklin Street, Fifth Floor, Boston, MA
02110-1301  USA
*/
class httpdServer extends socketServer {
}

class httpdServerClient extends socketServerClient {
    private $max_total_time = 45;
    private $max_idle_time  = 15;
    private $keep_alive = false;
    private $accepted;
    private $last_action;

    private function handle_request($request)
    {

        if (!$request['version'] || ($request['version'] != '1.0'
             && $request['version'] != '1.1')) {
          // sanity check on HTTP version
          $header = 'HTTP/'.$request['version']." 400 Bad Request\r\n";
          $output = '400: Bad request';
          $header .= "Content-Length: ".strlen($output)."\r\n";
        } elseif (!isset($request['method']) || ($request['method']
                   != 'get' && $request['method'] != 'post')) {
```

```php
      // sanity check on request method (only get and post are
allowed)
      $header  = 'HTTP/'.$request['version']." 400 Bad Request\r\n";
      $output  = '400: Bad request';
      $header .= "Content-Length: ".strlen($output)."\r\n";
    } else {
      // handle request
      if (empty($request['url'])) {
        $request['url'] = '/';
      }
      if ($request['url'] == '/' || $request['url'] == '') {
        $request['url'] = '/index.html';
      }
      // parse get params into $params variable
      if (strpos($request['url'],'?') !== false) {
        $params = substr($request['url'],
                    strpos($request['url'],'?') + 1);
        $params = explode('&', $params);
        foreach($params as $key => $param) {
          $pair = explode('=', $param);
          $params[$pair[0]] = isset($pair[1]) ? $pair[1] : '';
          unset($params[$key]);
        }
        $request['url'] = substr($request['url'], 0,
                    strpos($request['url'], '?'));
      }

      $file = './htdocs'.$request['url'];
      if (file_exists($file) && is_file($file)) {
        $header  = "HTTP/{$request['version']} 200 OK\r\n";
        $header .= "Accept-Ranges: bytes\r\n";
        $header .= 'Last-Modified: '.gmdate('D, d M Y H:i:s T',
                    filemtime($file))."\r\n";
        $size    = filesize($file);
        $header .= "Content-Length: $size\r\n";
        $output  = file_get_contents($file);
      } else {
        $output  = '<h1>404: Document not found.</h1>';
        $header  = "'HTTP/{$request['version']} 404 Not Found\r\n".
          "Content-Length: ".strlen($output)."\r\n";
      }
    }
    $header .= 'Date: '.gmdate('D, d M Y H:i:s T')."\r\n";
    if ($this->keep_alive) {
      $header .= "Connection: Keep-Alive\r\n";
```

```php
      $header .= "Keep-Alive: timeout={$this->max_idle_time}
                                max={$this->max_total_time}\r\n";
    } else {
      $this->keep_alive = false;
      $header .= "Connection: Close\r\n";
    }
    return $header."\r\n".$output;
  }

  public function on_read()
  {
    $this->last_action = time();
    if ((strpos($this->read_buffer,"\r\n\r\n")) !== FALSE ||
        (strpos($this->read_buffer,"\n\n")) !== FALSE) {
      $request = array();
      $headers = split("\n", $this->read_buffer);
      $request['uri'] = $headers[0];
      unset($headers[0]);
      while (list(, $line) = each($headers)) {
        $line = trim($line);
        if ($line != '') {
          $pos  = strpos($line, ':');
          $type = substr($line,0, $pos);
          $val  = trim(substr($line, $pos + 1));
          $request[strtolower($type)] = strtolower($val);
        }
      }
      $uri                 = $request['uri'];
      $request['method']   = strtolower(substr($uri, 0,
                             strpos($uri, ' ')));
      $request['version']  = substr($uri, strpos($uri, 'HTTP/')
                                                    + 5, 3);
      $uri                 = substr($uri, strlen($request['method']) + 1);
      $request['url']      = substr($uri, 0, strpos($uri, ' '));
      foreach ($request as $type => $val) {
        if ($type == 'connection' && $val == 'keep-alive') {
          $this->keep_alive = true;
        }
      }
      $this->write($this->handle_request($request));
      $this->read_buffer   = '';
    }
  }
```

```php
    public function on_connect()
    {
      //echo "[httpServerClient] accepted connection from
              {$this->remote_address}\n";
      $this->accepted    = time();
      $this->last_action = $this->accepted;
    }

    public function on_disconnect()
    {
      //echo "[httpServerClient] {$this->remote_address}
                                    disconnected\n";
    }

    public function on_write()
    {
      if (strlen($this->write_buffer) == 0 && !$this->keep_alive) {
        $this->disconnected = true;
        $this->on_disconnect();
        $this->close();
      }
    }

    public function on_timer()
    {
      $idle_time  = time() - $this->last_action;
      $total_time = time() - $this->accepted;
      if ($total_time > $this->max_total_time ||
          $idle_time > $this->max_idle_time) {
        echo "[httpServerClient] Client keep-alive time exceeded
                                  ({$this->remote_address})\n";
        $this->close();
      }
    }
  }
```

Technically speaking, we are required to implement each one of the class methods to handle the various inputs and outputs of our TCP server. While the example we just saw implements an HTTP server, it can be modified to handle FastAGI requests instead.

The following is a simple framework for creating an AGI server, using the `phpSocketDaemon` library:

## FastAGI.php:

```
#!/usr/bin/php -Cq
<?
/*
  A Simple FastAGI server using phpsocketserver.php
*/

    ini_set('mbstring.func_overload', '0');
    ini_set('output_handler', '');
    error_reporting(E_ALL | E_STRICT);
    @ob_end_flush();
    set_time_limit(0);
    include("socket.php");
    include("fastagiServer.php");

    $daemon = new socketDaemon();
    $server = $daemon->create_server('fastagiServer',
            'fastagiServerClient', 0, 4573);
    $daemon->process();
?>
```

Now, we need to create our `fastagiServer` class.

## fastagiServer.php:

```
<?
/*
  A Simple FastAGI server class for phpsocketserver.php
*/

class fastagiServer extends socketServer {

}

class fastagiServerClient extends socketServerClient {

    private $max_total_time = 45;
    private $max_idle_time  = 15;
    private $keep_alive = false;
    private $accepted;
    private $last_action;

    public function on_read() {
      // handle incomming data which is in $this->read_buffer,for
      // example the following looks for \r\n, then parses the complete
```

```
      // instruction to 'handle_request'
       .
       .
       .
    }
    public function on_connect() {
      // Invoked when a client connects to the binded port
       .
       .
       .
    }
    public function on_disconnect() {
      // Invoked when a connected client disconnects from the binded
      // port
       .
       .
       .
    }
    public function on_timer() {
      // Invoked upon a connected client's keep alive setting is
      // exceeded
       .
       .
       .
    }
}
```

At this point, you can surely imagine ways to incorporate the `PHPAGI` class library with the `phpsocketserver` class library, to enable a better PHP-based FastAGI server.

## FastAGI with other tool kits

As indicated earlier, PHP isn't the most native choice for writing FastAGI servers. PERL and Java are more popular for developing FastAGI servers. While the methodology is slightly different, the general concepts remain identical.

## Asterisk::FastAGI—a PERL module for FastAGI handling

Asterisk has several PERL modules for developing AGI scripts and FastAGI servers. While `Asterisk::AGI` provides a simple interface for AGI development, `Asterisk::FastAGI` provides a similar facility for FastAGI development.

> The `Asterisk::FastAGI` module is available from the CPAN repository.

`Asterisk::FastAGI` has become fairly popular for FastAGI development, as it handles the network and process forking by itself, freeing the developer from that task. The following is an example:

```
use base 'Asterisk::FastAGI';

sub fastagi_handler {
  my $self = shift;

  my $param = $self->param('foo');
  my $callerid = $self->input('calleridname');

  $self->agi->say_number(1000);
}
```

## Asterisk-JAVA—a Java package for Asterisk

Asterisk-Java has become highly popular over the past few years, as more and more Java developers have made the transition to Asterisk development. Asterisk-Java is fully compatible with versions 1.0, 1.2, 1.4 and 1.6 of Asterisk, and is an ideal candidate for code portability and compatibility.

The main drawback of using Asterisk-Java is Java, as it requires a hefty toll to be paid for using a Java core (in terms of complexity and performance—not financially).

However, thanks to Java's fairly simplistic networking and multi-threading abilities, Asterisk-Java has become the default choice for many developers for FastAGI server development.

> Asterisk-JAVA is available at http://www.asterisk-java.org.

While Asterisk-JAVA is at version 0.3 and is considered to be under constant development, it is highly stable and debugged.

## Summary

As we've learned so far, AGI and FastAGI provide for a highly versatile and robust programming environment for developing interactive voice applications. Each one has its own pros and cons. However, a balanced use of the two, combined with Asterisk's dialplan applications and functions, can make for a highly mature and flexible IVR framework.

An intresting question is raised at this point: "Can we interact with Asterisk outside the channel or the dialplan construct? Can we instruct Asterisk to perform a function without being in call at all?" The answer to these is: Yes, we can—by using the Asterisk Manager Interface.

At this point, we suggest that you take a short break from the book, in order to fully digest what you've learned so far. Try redeveloping your previously developed scripts as FastAGI servers, and get to learn the FastAGI mechanism better.

# 8
# AMI: The Asterisk Manager Interface

*The metaphor is perhaps one of man's most fruitful potentialities. Its efficacy verges on magic, and it seems a tool for creation which God forgot inside one of His creatures when He made him.*-Jose Ortega Y Gasset

Just like the Metaphor, **Asterisk Manager Interface (AMI)** is some kind of a magical thing, capable of performing highly complex telephony operations in a simple manner.

Judging from a technical point of view, the Manager Interface is one of the most simple devices that Asterisk can offer to the developer. However, even though it is simple and straightforward, it is also a pivotal point for applications, which if developed incorrectly, could generate a completely different set of results.

Understanding the capabilities and constraints of using the AMI interface is the key to developing AMI-aware applications. This chapter will get you up and running with AMI.

## AMI—the history

The AMI Interface was available with Asterisk almost from day one. Its initial use was a means for obtaining runtime information about Asterisk's runtime environment. As time progressed, the AMI interface slowly expanded, and additional functions were added to it. One of the pitfalls of AMI is its lack of proper documentation. Thus, AMI is a set of highly undocumented events and actions, sometimes yielding a slightly different result from the one you expect.

## How does AMI work?

The AMI interface is actually a TCP server, which is automatically executed with Asterisk and is connected directly to the Asterisk core. As calls are passed through the Asterisk core, the AMI interface will emit events to any TCP client connected to the AMI TCP server.

Like any other portion of Asterisk, the AMI interface is controlled by a specific configuration file, in our case, /etc/asterisk/manager.conf.

```
manager.conf:
;
; Asterisk Call Management support
;
[general]
enabled = yes
port = 5038
bindaddr = 0.0.0.0

[amiclient]
secret = amiclient111
deny=0.0.0.0/0.0.0.0
permit=127.0.0.1/255.255.255.0
read = system,call,log,verbose,command,agent,user
write = system,call,log,verbose,command,agent,user
```

> By default, the AMI interface is not enabled. If your applications require AMI functionality, you should enable it via the configuration file.

Like any other Asterisk configuration file, the manager.conf file is made up of configuration contexts. While the [general] context is fairly simple, every other context simply defines the various AMI access users and their permissions.

Pay special attention to the port and enabled parameters. By default, the enabled parameters will be set to no, disabling the Asterisk Manager. The port parameter indicates which TCP port to bind the Asterisk Manager to—5038 being the default one.

The following context—amiclient— specifies the username that is allowed to connect to the Asterisk Manager. Pay special attention to the fact that usernames and secrets (aka: passwords) are case sensitive.

A connected AMI user may connect from hosts or networks defined in the `permit` configuration directive. Note that the following example denies access from the Internet (0.0.0.0/0.0.0.0) and permits access only from specific hosts or networks:

```
deny=0.0.0.0/0.0.0.0
permit=127.0.0.1/255.255.255.0
```

Once we have defined our access list, we are required to predefine a set of events and actions that our user is allowed to access. This is defined using the `read` and `write` directive. While `read` indicates that the events of the types indicated are sent to the connected AMI user, the `write` directive indicates that the AMI interface will allow the user to initiate actions for these types of events only.

The following is a short explanation of the information available for each of these event/action types:

- system: Actions and events related to Asterisk's core elements, such as SIP peers and the Asterisk Database
- call: Actions and events related directly to Asterisk's extension statuses, and call progress and call control
- log: The source documentation doesn't provide detailed information about the nature of information provided by events of this type.
- verbose: The source documentation doesn't provide detailed information about the nature of information provided by events of this type.
- command: This directive enables our connected user to send commands to the Asterisk CLI interface
- Agent: Actions and events related to Asterisk's queue applications
- User: User events can be generated from the dialplan, using the `UserEvent` application. Using user events are a valuable tool when developing applications that incorporate dialplan, AGI, and AMI at the same time.

> It would be fair to say that by the time this book gets published, additional commands and events will have been added to the Asterisk Manager. It would be a good practice to dig into the Asterisk code documentation and learn what has been added and/or modified.

## AMI with Asterisk 1.0 and 1.2

In the early days of Asterisk, the AMI interface was one of Asterisk's main pitfalls. The main reason for this pitfall was its single-threaded nature. Thus, users connected to the AMI interface ran into serious deadlocks, especially when trying to both read and write information into the manager interface at the same time.

## AMI with Asterisk 1.4 and 1.6

Asterisk version 1.4, and its successor 1.6 have introduced a major rewrite to some of the AMI interface servers, thereby allowing multi-threaded operations and better flow control over connected users. The chances of running into a deadlock still exist, however, these have become fairly rare in these versions.

## AMI–understanding basics

Before any interaction with the AMI interface can be performed, the user must first need to log in to the manager interface. The simplest way to illustrate this is using the 'telnet' application. Simply initiate a telnet to the Asterisk Manager Interface, and you will be greeted with the following:

```
[root@venus ~]# telnet 127.0.0.1 5038
Trying 127.0.0.1...
Connected to localhost.localdomain (127.0.0.1).
Escape character is '^]'.
Asterisk Call Manager/1.0
```

From this point onwards, the AMI interface expects you to interact without using text-based commands, as described by the interface.

> Please note that if you are using Asterisk version 1.6 or SVN, Asterisk Manager's version is 1.1 and not 1.0.

## Events and Actions

The Asterisk Manager provides two main facilities of communications—events and actions. Events are invoked by the various parts of Asterisk, be it channel drivers, applications, resources, or any other component connected directly to the Asterisk core. The purpose of an **event** is to enable an external system to obtain information from Asterisk, by collecting these events, parsing them, correlating them, and initiating actions in accordance with these events. **Actions** provide a method of allowing an external system to send operational commands to Asterisk, asking it to perform a specific task. While an action may result in true operational results (such as originating an outbound call), it may also result in new events being sent to the Asterisk Manager with new information.

## Logging in to the Manager Interface

The first thing we'll need to do is to actually log in to the interface, using the `login` action. Simply type the following text into your connected AMI interface:

```
Action: login
Username: admin
Secret: god
```

Please note that after the last line of input, you will be required to press your *Enter* key again, as the AMI interface requires an empty line feed at the end of the input, to indicate that the input has been completed (if you are familiar with SMTP servers, this doesn't seem all that weird).

Another variant would be to add the `Events: off` directive, after the `Secret` directive. This will tell the AMI interface not to send manager events to your connected user.

## Sending actions to the Manager Interface

An action comprises an action directive, a set of keys, and variables (if required). The format of an action request is as follows:

```
Action: <action type><CRLF>
<Key 1>: <Value 1><CRLF>
<Key 2>: <Value 2><CRLF>
...
Variable: <Variable 1>=<Value 1><CRLF>
Variable: <Variable 2>=<Value 2><CRLF>
...
<CRLF>
```

The following is a small example of an Asterisk Manager action that includes some variables and keys:

```
Action: Originate
Channel: SIP/203
Context: default
Exten: 204
Priority: 1
Callerid: 203
Variable: call_originator=jollyroger
```

The above example will generate a call to the SIP device, registered as `203`. Once the SIP device `203` picks up, Asterisk will then direct the connected channel to the `default` context, trying to dial extension number `204`. The variable `call_originator` is set to `jollyroger` and may be used later on within the Asterisk dialplan.

## Logging off from the Manager Interface

Once you have completed your interaction with the AMI interface, simply log off. While some developers may argue that this is redundant, it is good practice to close the connection properly and indicate a logoff from the manager, as in some application cases this may be a requirement (especially in a call center or contact center scenario). Simply type the following text into your connected AMI interface:

```
Action: logoff
```

The response from the AMI interface should be as follows:

```
Response: Goodbye
Message: Thanks for all the fish.
```

> Off topic: If the term "Thanks for all the fish" seems weird for this point, we suggest that you read Douglas Adams's *The Hitch Hiker's Guide to the Galaxy*. You will also find out that the universal truth is 42, but that's a completely different thing.

## PHPAGI and the AMI Interface

PHPAGI includes a class library for interacting easily with the AMI interface. In order to utilize the AMI interface with PHPAGI, we must first configure our AMI login information in the `phpagi.conf` file. The following is an example, according to the `amiclient` configuration example seen previously:

```
[asmanager]
server=192.168.80.130    ; server to connect to
port=5038                ; default manager port
username=amiclient       ; username for login
secret= amiclient111     ; password for login
```

Once you have configured your AMI interface information, you are required to initiate the Asterisk Manager class from your PHP script. This is available in two different methods—invoking the AMI interface class directly from its own class, or invoking it via the PHPAGI class library.

## Direct AMI interface invocation

The following code snippet shows how to invoke the AMI interface directly:

```
1.   <?
2.
3.   $BASE_PATH="/var/lib/asterisk/agi-bin/";
```

```
4.
5.     require $BASE_PATH."../php-common/phpagi.php";
6.     /* your script does some stuff here */
7.     .
8.     .
9.     /* Now we connect to the AMI interface */
10.    $astManager = new AGI_AsteriskManager();
11.    $res = $astManager->connect($ast_host, $ast_user, $ast_pass);
12.    if(!$res) {
13.        syslog(LOG_INFO, "Connection to Asterisk manager failed.");
14.        die(100);
15.    }
16.    /* Now we do some manager stuff here */
17.    .
18.    .
19.    /* Now we close the connection and logout */
20.    $astManager->disconnect();
21.
22. ?>
```

The code snippet just seen tries to connect to the manager interface (lines 10-11). If the connection is unsuccessful (lines 12-15), the script will simply die and return a value of 100 to the operating system.

Once we are connected to the AMI interface, we can interface with it.

## AMI interface invocation via the PHPAGI class

The following code snippet shows how to invoke the AMI interface directly:

```
1.  <?
2.
3.     $BASE_PATH="/var/lib/asterisk/agi-bin/";
4.
5.     require $BASE_PATH."../php-common/phpagi.php";
6.     /* your script does some stuff here */
7.     .
8.     .
9.     /* Now we connect to the AMI interface */
10.    $agiWrapper = new AGI ();
11.    $astManager = $agiWrapper->new_AsteriskManager*();
12.    $res = $astManager->connect($ast_host, $ast_user, $ast_pass);
13.    if(!$res) {
14.        syslog(LOG_INFO, "Connection to Asterisk manager failed.");
15.        die(100);
```

```
16.      }
17.      /* Now we do some manager stuff here */
18.      .
19.      .
20.      /* Now we close the connection and logout */
21.      $astManager->disconnect();
22.
23. ?>
```

This code snippet invokes the AGI class. Once invoked, it initiates an Asterisk Manager interface via the `new_AsteriskManager` method (lines 10-11). As before, we first validate that our manager connection is available, and if not, we simply kill our script with a return value of `100` (lines 13-16).

## Interacting with the AMI interface

Once our AMI interface is connected, we need to interact with it. Interaction is performed via actions and events. In order to initiate an action, we are required to utilize the `send_request` method. In order to trigger events correctly, we are required to create handling functions and declare these as event callbacks.

## Sending actions to the AMI inteface

Sending an action to the AMI interface once connected, using the `send_request` method, is very simple. The `send_request` directive syntax is as follows:

```
$as->send_request($eventname, $arrayofparameterstopass);
```

Here `$as` specifies your AMI interface object. The next is a short example of how this is done:

```
$res = $as->send_request('EventName',
                    array('Channel'=>'Zap/1/16045551212',
                          'SomeParameter'=>'data'));
echo "Dump of returned data:\n";

foreach($res as $var=>$val) echo "$var = $val\n";
```

The above code sends an action called `EventName` followed by the parameters detailed by the array in the `send_request` method.

# Event callbacks from AMI interface

As events are fired from the AMI to our program, we sometimes need to process these events. PHPAGI enables a methodology of defining various handling functions, and then attaching these functions to specific events via a callback facility.

For example, let's imagine that we'd like to add an event handler for an event called `Dial`, indicating that a call was just dialed from a certain source to a specific channel.

```
<?
.
.
function evt_dial($ecode, $data, $server, $port) {
   /* Do something here */
}

$astManager->add_event_handler('dial','evt_dial');
.
.
?>
```

If you would like to create a catch all event, simply define the * event handler. For example:

```
<?
.
.
function evt_all($ecode, $data, $server, $port) {
   /* Do some thing here */
}

$astManager->add_event_handler('*','evt_all');
.
.
?>
```

In the above case, any event generated will automatically invoke the `evt_all` function.

> Events are processed using a block socket. This means that as events are processed, your code will not be able to execute additional actions to the AMI interface. If you want to be able to read events and send actions independently, make sure you use two different connections for this, with different sets of permissions.

# PHPAGI AMI originate quirk

As we've learned before, PHPAGI was initially developed to be compatible with Asterisk versions 1.0 and 1.2. One of the actions that has changed slightly from version 1.2 of Asterisk to its later versions is the Originate action.

The Originate action is used to instruct Asterisk to initiate a call to a pre-defined channel and then connect the call to an Asterisk dialplan context. The Originate action is commonly used in phone callback scenarios, call center and contact center dialers, and alerting systems.

To be more precise, the thing that changed wasn't the action itself, but how Asterisk deciphers the variables provided to the Originate action. However, in order to understand the quirk, let's first examine the Originate action. The following is a direct extract from the Asterisk code base (extracted from manager.c):

```
static char mandescr_originate[] =
"Description: Generates an outgoing call to a Extension/Context/
Priority or\n"
"  Application/Data\n"
"Variables: (Names marked with * are required)\n"
"  *Channel: Channel name to call\n"
"  Exten: Extension to use (requires 'Context' and 'Priority')\n"
"  Context: Context to use (requires 'Exten' and 'Priority')\n"
"  Priority: Priority to use (requires 'Exten' and 'Context')\n"
"  Application: Application to use\n"
"  Data: Data to use (requires 'Application')\n"
"  Timeout: How long to wait for call to be answered (in ms)\n"
"  CallerID: Caller ID to be set on the outgoing channel\n"
"  Variable: Channel variable to set, multiple Variable: headers are allowed\n"
"  Account: Account code\n"
"  Async: Set to 'true' for fast origination\n";
```

The mandatory action key is Channel, because when originating a call we are originating it from a specific channel. The interesting part here is the information passed to the Variable key, and how these variables are parsed. Examination of the manager.c code indicates that the variables are parsed using the ast_variable function.

The key difference is that while versions 1.0 and 1.2 used the pipe (|) symbol as a variable separator, in versions 1.4 and 1.6 of Asterisk, we are required to enter multiple Variable lines, instead of using a variable separator.

This distinct difference poses an issue when sending an Originate event via the pre-canned Originate manager action with PHPAGI. Let's now take a look at the PHPAGI pre-canned Originate action code:

## phpagi-asmanager.php—Originate function

```
/**
* Originate Call
*
* @link
*  http://www.voip-info.org/wiki-Asterisk+Manager+API+Action+Originate
* @param string $channel Channel name to call
* @param string $exten Extension to use (requires 'Context' and
* 'Priority')
* @param string $context Context to use (requires 'Exten' and
* 'Priority')
* @param string $priority Priority to use (requires 'Exten' and
* 'Context')
* @param string $application Application to use
* @param string $data Data to use (requires 'Application')
* @param integer $timeout How long to wait for call to be
*  answered (in ms)
* @param string $callerid Caller ID to be set on the outgoing
*  channel
* @param string $variable Channel variable to set
* (VAR1=value1|VAR2=value2)
* @param string $account Account code
* @param boolean $async true fast origination
* @param string $actionid message matching variable
*/
function Originate($channel,
    $exten=NULL, $context=NULL, $priority=NULL,
    $application=NULL, $data=NULL,
    $timeout=NULL, $callerid=NULL, $variable=NULL,
    $account=NULL, $async=NULL, $actionid=NULL)
{
  $parameters = array('Channel'=>$channel);

  if($exten) $parameters['Exten'] = $exten;
  if($context) $parameters['Context'] = $context;
  if($priority) $parameters['Priority'] = $priority;

  if($application) $parameters['Application'] = $application;
  if($data) $parameters['Data'] = $data;
```

```
    if($timeout) $parameters['Timeout'] = $timeout;
    if($callerid) $parameters['CallerID'] = $callerid;
    if($variable) $parameters['Variable'] = $variable;
    if($account) $parameters['Account'] = $account;
    if(!is_null($async)) $parameters['Async'] =
        ($async) ? 'true' : 'false';
    if($actionid) $parameters['ActionID'] = $actionid;

    return $this->send_request('Originate', $parameters);
}
```

As you can see, the PHPAGI `Originate` action function expects to receive the variables as a single string, and not as a full set of `Variable` directives.

In order to bypass this limitation, we shall simply construct our variables set as a single string, separated by the `\r\n` combination. For example, the following `Originate` method will be compatible with versions 1.0 and 1.2, while the latter will be compatible with versions 1.4 and 1.6.

## PHPAGI Originate for versions 1.0 and 1.2

```
$res = $astManager->Originate(
    'SIP/Vonage/12127773456', /* The channel          */
    '1001',         /* The Extension to connect       */
    'MyContext',    /* The Extension context          */
    1,              /* The Extension Priority         */
    NULL,           /* The application to use         */
    NULL,           /* The data for the application   */
    120000,         /* Timeout for answer in msec     */
    '1732557799',   /* The caller ID to use           */
    'var1=1|var2=3|var3=book', /* variables           */
    NULL,           /* Account code to assign         */
    0,              /* 1 for fast origination         */
    NULL)           /* Action ID for the originate    */
```

## PHPAGI Originate for versions 1.4 and 1.6

```
$res = $astManager->Originate(
    'SIP/Vonage/12127773456', /* The channel          */
    '1001',         /* The Extension to connect       */
    'MyContext',    /* The Extension context          */
    1,              /* The Extension Priority         */
    NULL,           /* The application to use         */
    NULL,           /* The data for the application   */
    120000,         /* Timeout for answer in msec     */
    '1732557799',   /* The caller ID to use           */
```

```
         'var1=1\r\nVariable: var2=3\r\nVariable: var3=book',
                  /* variables                */
    NULL,         /* Account code to assign   */
    0,            /* 1 for fast origination   */
    NULL)         /* Action ID for the originate */
```

## Asynchronous Originate actions

One of the most confusing keys of the `Originate` action is the `Async` key. While the documentation says: "For the origination to be asynchronous (that is allowing multiple calls to be generated without waiting for a response)", it leaves out a very important fact. Setting your `Originate` action to `Async=1` will always return a success for your `Originate` action, freeing the manager to handle another action.

This means that `Async=1` will result in a fast `Originate`, however a less reliable one, as you will be required to check the status of your `Originate` action using another method.

# Click-2-Call and Web-Callback

If you are a telephony developer, the previous section may have surely brought the following ideas and thoughts to your head: "Asterisk AMI interface includes an originate function, allowing me to generate outbound calls. Wouldn't it be cool to create an Asterisk-based click-2-call/callback application? But the question is—HOW?"

Creating a reliable callback/click-2-call application with Asterisk is one of the best kept secrets of this business. In fact, companies like JAJAH, HeyCosmo, and others, have raised considerable amount of cash from the idea of using Asterisk's originate action in creative ways.

# Demystifying the Asterisk Originate manager action

The `Originate` action expects to receive the following information:

```
   *Channel: Channel name to call
       Exten: Extension to use (requires 'Context' and 'Priority')
     Context: Context to use (requires 'Exten' and 'Priority')
    Priority: Priority to use (requires 'Exten' and 'Context')
 Application: Application to use
        Data: Data to use (requires 'Application')
     Timeout: How long to wait for call to be answered (in ms)
    CallerID: Caller ID to be set on the outgoing channel
```

```
   Variable: Channel variable to set, multiple Variable: headers are
             allowed
    Account: Account code
      Async: Set to 'true' for fast origination
```

From Asterisk's point of view, the only mandatory variable is the `Channel` variable. While the others are not mandatory, careful use of them will facilitate the creation of a callback/click-2-call functionality.

By defining the `Exten`, `Context`, and `Priority` variables, we provide Asterisk a dialplan routing point for our originated channel, to be connected to, once the called `Channel` has been answered. This means that if we originate with the following information:

```
*Channel: SIP/Vonage/12127773456
   Exten: 12127773456
 Context: movie-phone-crawler
Priority: 1
```

Asterisk will originate a call to the phone indicated in the channel. Once the call is connected, it will route the call to the `movie-phone-crawler` context, with extension number `12127773456` set at priority `1`.

This seems simple enough. So, how do we create a web-based click-2-call application, similar to what JAJAH has?

# Welcome to Jabka—the world's favourite Click-2-Call

Jabka is a prepaid web-based Click-2-Call application, allowing users from around the world to connect two telephone numbers via the service. The web developers have indicated that in order to initiate a call, they will be sending the following variables to your Asterisk application, according to the following XML-RPC scheme:

```xml
<?xml version="1.0" encoding="UTF-8"?>
<methodCall>
   <methodName>jbk.init_callback</methodName>
    <struct>
         <member>
              <name>session</name>
              <value><string>MD5_SESSION_HASH</string></value>
         </member>
         <member>
              <name>origination_number</name>
              <value><string>ORIGIN_NUMBER_TO_CALL</string></value>
```

```
                </member>
        <member>
                <name>target_number</name>
                <value><string>TARGET_NUMBER_TO_CALL</string></value>
                </member>
        <member>
                <name>max_duration</name>
                <value><int>MAX_DURATION_FOR_CALL_IN_mSEC
                </int></value>
                </member>
        </struct>
</methodCall>
```

> If you are unfamiliar with XML-RPC, please visit the
> http://www.xmlrpc.org website for additional information.

According to the above, we basically receive four parameters—the origin of the call, the target of the call, the maximum duration, and a session hash—which is more than enough. Now, let's translate this into an Originate request (we shall assume that all the channels will be based on SIP going to the Vonage SIP peer):

```
Action: Originate
Channel: SIP/Vonage/%origination_number%
Context: jabka-dial-target
Exten: %target_number%
Priority: 1
Timeout: 120000
Variable: maximumtime=%max_duration%
```

Ok, so we originate a call to the number indicated by origination_number and then connect to the jabka-dial-target context with the remaining information. Let's examine the jabka-dial-target context:

```
[jabka-dial-target]
exten => _X.,1,Noop(Starting Callback)
exten => _X.,n,Dial(SIP/Vonage/${EXTEN},120,rL(${max_duration}))

exten => h,1,Noop(Notify Billing System)
exten => h,n,DeadAGI(Your_CDR_and_Billing_AGI_Go_Here)
```

That's it! We're more or less done, as this is the basic structure.

You are most probably wondering to yourself that, if it's so simple, why doesn't everybody do it? Well, while the basic structure is fairly simple and straightforward, creating a full-blown service out of what we have just seen is slightly more problematic.

The Manager's unique manner of operations introduces interesting problems and challenges (which are way beyond the scope of this book). The various billing aspects and user flow aspects that need to be met are as important as the application itself; in other words, plan your application carefully.

## AMI proxy servers

As indicated previously in this chapter, if you are using versions of Asterisk prior to 1.4, you may run into deadlock issues when using the AMI interface. These issues can be resolved by using an AMI proxy server. Generally speaking, you would be required to work via some form of AMI proxy in every situation you interact with the AMI.

As you may have already figured out, the AMI interface emits messages for almost any type of event that occurs during the traversal of a call via an Asterisk server. While this is a required behavior, it can surely generate a multitude of messages when dealing with high capacity systems, such as call centers, for example. The purpose of the AMI proxy server is to filter out the events that are relevant for our use, pass these to our application, and subsequently, pass information from the application back to the AMI interface in an orderly fashion.

AMI Proxy servers are available from the Asterisk community, in various programming languages and with varied performance and feature sets. Whatever be the proxy server you choose, make sure you verify that it is the correct one for you.

> Developing a proxy server for AMI is beyond the scope of this book, as a proxy needs to be tailored to suit your requirements. To read more information about AMI Proxy servers, please refer to the voip-info Asterisk Manager Proxy page, located at: http://www.voip-info.org/wiki-Asterisk+Manager+Proxy.

## AJAM—AJAX Enabled Manager

As Asterisk has evolved, so have web technologies. With the introduction of Asterisk 1.4 to the world, a new method of interfacing with the Asterisk Manager was created. This new method combines the somewhat simple manner of meshing Web 2.0 applications via JavaScript with the fierce abilities of the Asterisk Manager. The newly-created interface was named **AJAM** (**Asynchronous JavaScript Asterisk Manager**).

> Some people argue that AJAM stands for AJAX Asterisk Manager, which makes for one of the world's longest acronyms: **Asynchronous JavaScript and XML Asterisk Manager**.

AJAM is a standard part of Asterisk 1.4 and onwards. However, its not activated by default. As this book is concentrating on PHP and AGI, we won't go neck-deep into the AJAM interface. To find out additional information about AJAM, the best place to start your quest would be the voip-info website, at: `http://www.voip-info.org/wiki/view/Aynchronous+Javascript+Asterisk+Manager+(AJAM)`.

The AsteriskGUI used in versions 1.0.2 of AsteriskNOW and some other Asterisk-based applications relies heavily on AJAM to perform its functions.

## Summary

Congratulations! You have now mastered both the basic and advanced concepts of developing IVR/CTI applications with Asterisk—the open source PBX. At this point, your mind is most probably racing with ideas and thoughts of how to apply your new know-how to create new applications.

Before you go on and develop your own application, we suggest that you take a day's leave from this book, and return to Chapter 9 later. Chapter 9 will describe a project for you to develop, which will allow you to better practise all that you've learned.

# 9
# Final Programming Project

Welcome to the final programming project. The purpose of this project is to introduce to you a project, that has already been developed, and to let you go through the various requirements and develop the solution on your own.

There is no solution provided for this final project, as the purpose of this project is to make you think, code, debug, and to better understand the Asterisk AGI/AMI development structures.

While this book has introduced all the topics using the PHP programming language and the PHPAGI class library, you may utilize whatever programming language you like and utilize whatever tools you may require. Anything goes!

The project described can be developed by an experienced developer in not more than two weeks. My assumption is that it may take you up to three weeks to develop it.

> If you decide to implement the project and run into problems, feel free to contact me at `asteriskdevbook@greenfieldtech.net`, or via the support forums at `http://www.greenfieldtech.net/support`.
>
> **Personal Note:**
> If you have completed the project, and you are feeling mighty proud of yourself (more than you should), I urge you to send me your solution via email, so I can go over it, and if possible, give you a few pointers as to whether you could have done it better. If I find your solution to be perfect as is, it will be published in my website with a credit to you, for all to see.

*Final Programming Project*

# ACRG—Asterisk Call Recording Gateway

Call recording systems are being used by call centers and contact centers around the world. No matter whether it's an ISP technical support center or a bank's stock market trading center, call recording is essential for monitoring and assurance purposes. Companies such as Verint and NICE have made it their business to provide highly reliable call and transaction recordings, thereby building solutions that can cost up to hundreds of thousands of dollars. Our intention is to enable similar capabilities with Asterisk at a much lower cost.

## Requirements

You are required to provide a solution for recording calls, as they traverse a "call recording" gateway that you will develop. Calls may traverse the recording gateway in either TDM or VoIP technology, as supported by the Asterisk Open PBX System.

The Call Recording Gateway shall support the following features:

- Transparent call recording of calls into a single audio file; both channels shall be recorded to the same file
- All calls should be logged to a centralized database, such as MySQL or Oracle
- All recordings should be saved to `/var/lib/asterisk/sounds/archive`
- Recordings should be available for retrieval via a web interface
- All recordings should be saved in the MP3 file format
- The recording system should provide an HTTP-based API for retrieval of calls, without interaction with the recording system database
- The recording system should allow the manager to specify which calls to record and which aren't supposed to be recorded, depending on the CallerID of the call
- The recording system should be able to record up to 120 concurrent calls
- All calls should be uniquely identified
- The recording system should provide full logging and debugging information via syslog

# Network connectivity—PSTN

Due to the nature of call recording and the fact that we can't record an E1/T1 circuit without interfacing with it (at least not without additional hardware), our call recording system will be interconnected with the existing PSTN and PBX system in accordance with the following diagram.

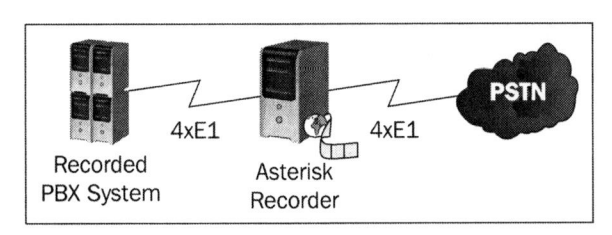

While the diagram shows E1 circuits, the recording system should be able to utilize the same structure of connectivity for T1 circuits or VoIP connectivity.

# Project implementation guide

Every project should be split into several distinct steps. While each software development and project management methodology may define different steps, the following are the minimum number of steps required to implement our project.

- **Step 1: Analysis of the requirements**
  In my view, this is the most crucial part of the project flow, as every other step is a direct derivative of this one. The analysis stage should contain a complete investigation of the platform's requirements, the possible pitfalls, and more importantly, the possible implementation paths to be taken.
  If your project requires the utilization of multiple business entities or departments, this would be the time to identify the various critical paths in the implementation.

- **Step 2: Understanding operational constraints**
  Understanding the operational constraints can be described as: "knowing your game field". Each computing and hardware environment will impose a different set of constraints on your developed system. Be it the operating system, file system, hardware, or network constraints, these should be evaluated at this point, and proper solution methodologies should be devised. If step 1 has identified multiple critical paths, it would be advisable to allow a step to evaluate the operational constraint of each path (if required), and deal with each of these independent of the others.

- **Step 3: Detailed call flow charts**
  We are dealing with a telephony system, so we must take into consideration the general feel of the system from the user's point of view. Describing this using a flow chart is the simplest and the fastest way to do so. Don't dwell too much on the semantics of the flow chart; sometimes even a simple block diagram will be enough for a developer to understand what you want.

- **Step 4: The Asterisk dialplan**
  By finalizing steps 2 and 3, we should already have a clear view of what Asterisk is supposed to do—at least for the dialplan portion of the project. This would be a good place to start developing the system. If you are required (and you most probably are) to develop AGI scripts, creating AGI stubs and inserting them into the proper dialplan locations will allow you for rapid development and prototyping. Always test your dialplan as you develop it; this will shorten your QA time in step 6.

- **Step 5: Human interface development**
  If you require the development of human interfaces (usually web-based), these can be developed in parallel to your voice application. Make sure you use a well-proven, well-documented framework to develop your human interface; it will make life easier in the testing step.

- **Step 6: Test, test, and test again**
  Devise proper testing procedures for your system, based on the specifications and analysis provided in steps 1 and 2. Bear in mind that your system should do what it's supposed to do, and not other things. Remember, sometimes better is worse than good.

> To learn more about critical path and constraint-based project and development management, please refer a book named: *Critical Chain* by Eliyahu M. Goldrat. The "Critical Chain" theory is part of a greater theory called **The Theory of Constraints**, and it has helped me finish projects and developments much faster in the past—thanks to a clearer view of what projects are.

Now let's see each step in great detail.

# Step 1: Analysis of the requirements

The ACRG project requires that we utilize several components that are not a part of Asterisk, mainly, a database server for logging all the calls and an MP3 encoder to encode our recordings in MP3 format.

While the use of a database server is fairly simple, the conversion to MP3 isn't. It would seem fairly natural that Asterisk should be fully capable of recording MP3 files. However, this is not the case. Due to various license restrictions, Asterisk includes an MP3 file playback ability (via the Asterisk-addons package), but not MP3 recording capabilities. This dictates that we need to use an external MP3 encoder—LAME in our case.

> The LAME project website is available at http://lame.sourceforge.net/. If you are using any of the well-known distributions (Fedora, Ubuntu, SUSE, and so on), you should have a LAME package available via your distribution. It is better, for the sake of simplicity, to use the pre-packaged version that came with your distribution of Linux, rather than compile your own.

Another issue that needs to be taken into account is the fact that encoding files from WAV to MP3 requires CPU resources. A recording system can easily have any number of calls running concurrently, depending on its overall capacity. This means that if my system has to record 120 channels, statistically speaking, at any given time I may have 30-40 recordings ready to be encoded. If you try to encode multiple MP3 files, you would notice that the CPU will most probably spike, and will result in a generally degraded performance across the entire server.

## Step 2: Understanding operational constraints

As we've described before, one of our main constraints is the resources required for converting a WAV file to an MP3 file. However, we have two more constraints that are as important as the conversion—file system utilization, and structure and database indexes.

Let's discuss the issue of file system utilization and structure first. As you may or may not know, any file system has a preset number of constraints, which, if surpassed, will make the file system slow or completely unusable. For example, Linux by default uses the EXT3 file system. While EXT3 is a perfect file system for anything that has to be done, it cannot effectively deal with thousands of file entries in a single directory.

> Actually, one of the built-in recording interfaces that is available with FreePBX/TrixBox is called **ARI** (**Asterisk Recording Interface**). ARI has a web interface that interacts directly with the file system. When the file system reaches a number of over 3000 recordings, the ARI interface becomes unresponsive.

# Final Programming Project

So, our aim is to create a directory + file structure that will enable us to better utilize our file system constraints. The following diagram illustrates a directory structure that will enable an extendable directory structure, while ensuring that we don't surpass our file system limitations (at least within normal operational conditions).

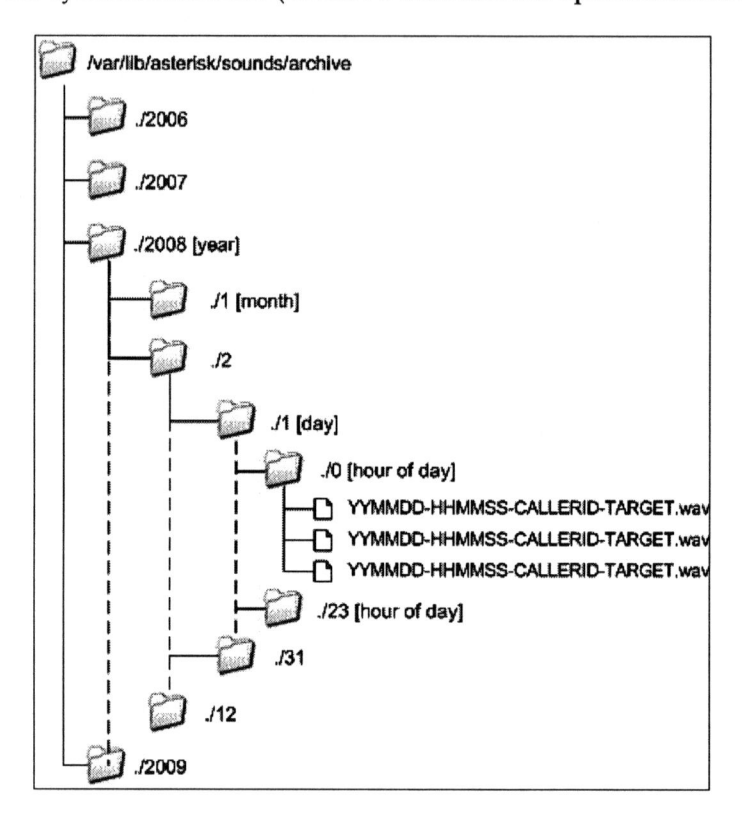

```
/var/lib/asterisk/sounds/archive
├── ./2006
├── ./2007
├── ./2008 [year]
│   ├── ./1 [month]
│   ├── ./2
│   │   ├── ./1 [day]
│   │   │   ├── ./0 [hour of day]
│   │   │   │   ├── YYMMDD-HHMMSS-CALLERID-TARGET.wav
│   │   │   │   ├── YYMMDD-HHMMSS-CALLERID-TARGET.wav
│   │   │   │   └── YYMMDD-HHMMSS-CALLERID-TARGET.wav
│   │   │   └── ./23 [hour of day]
│   │   └── ./31
│   └── ./12
└── ./2009
```

The above diagram illustrates a directory structure in which each year is represented by a directory, followed by the number of month in a year. Each month directory contains further directories for the days of the month. The directory for each day will contain up to twenty-four different directories, each one indicating a discrete hour of the day.

The file-naming convention of the recordings is as follows:

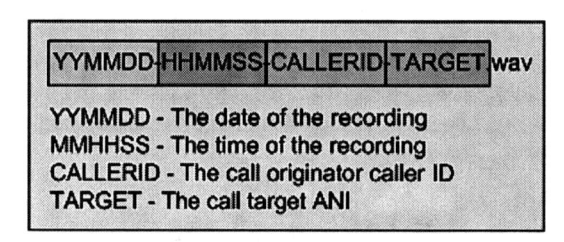

`YYMMDD-HHMMSS-CALLERID-TARGET.wav`

YYMMDD - The date of the recording
MMHHSS - The time of the recording
CALLERID - The call originator caller ID
TARGET - The call target ANI

The directory structure and the file naming convention shown in the immediately preceding diagram, allow us to navigate the file system easily and identify each recording uniquely, yet preserving a highly simplistic structure, readable to most people, including those who are not computer savvy.

Now that we have addressed our directory and file structure constraint, we can approach our database constraint.

If you have ever had to work with a DBA, you may have surely noticed that DBAs tend to be highly protective of their indexes. The indexes of a database table may sometimes dictate whether the application is usable or completely useless. A recording system needs to register each call into the **CDR (Call Detail Record)** table and the recordings table. However, it must go about and maintain a proper set of indexes, so that we are able to query and filter these tables in an efficient manner.

The following diagram illustrates a possible structure for the recordings table in the database:

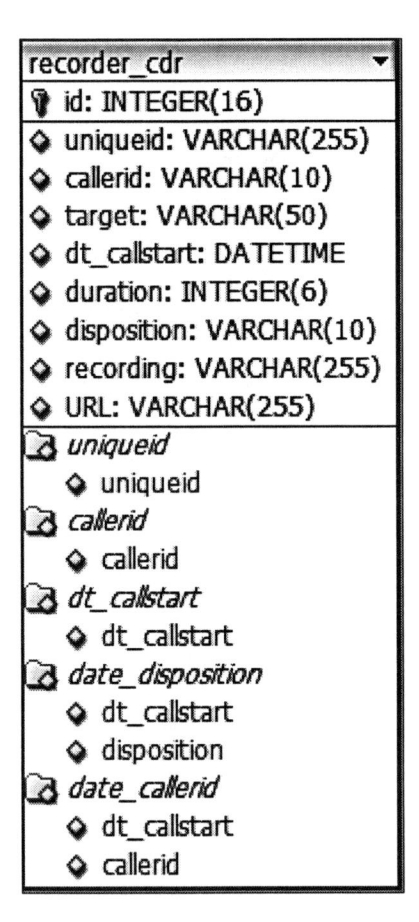

```
recorder_cdr
🔑 id: INTEGER(16)
◇ uniqueid: VARCHAR(255)
◇ callerid: VARCHAR(10)
◇ target: VARCHAR(50)
◇ dt_callstart: DATETIME
◇ duration: INTEGER(6)
◇ disposition: VARCHAR(10)
◇ recording: VARCHAR(255)
◇ URL: VARCHAR(255)
📇 uniqueid
    ◇ uniqueid
📇 callerid
    ◇ callerid
📇 dt_callstart
    ◇ dt_callstart
📇 date_disposition
    ◇ dt_callstart
    ◇ disposition
📇 date_callerid
    ◇ dt_callstart
    ◇ callerid
```

*Final Programming Project*

As you may notice from the immdiately previous diagram, our `recorder_cdr` table contains the following fields:

| Field name | Field type | Description |
|---|---|---|
| id | INTEGER(16) | Numerical sequence ID |
| Uniqueid | VARCHAR(255) | Hash identifier for the recording |
| Callerid | VARCHAR(10) | The caller ID of the recording |
| Target | VARCHAT(50) | The target ANI number |
| Dt_callstart | Datetime | The date and time of the call start |
| Duration | INTEGER(6) | The duration of the call in seconds |
| Disposition | VARCHAR(10) | The disposition status of the call |
| Recording | VARCHAR(255) | The location of the recording in the file system |
| URL | VARCHAR(255) | A URL identifier where the recording can be retrieved from using the web server |

While the table fields are more or less understandable, we need to take a look at the indexes of the table:

| Index | Field of Index | Description |
|---|---|---|
| Uniqueid | Uniqueid | An index according to the unique hash identifier of a specific recording |
| Callerid | Callerid | An index according to the caller ID of the recording |
| Dt_callstart | Dt_callstart | An index according to the date and time of the recording |
| Date_disposition | Dt_callstart disposition | An index according to the date and time of the recording, intersected with the recording's disposition |
| Date_callerid | Dt_callstart callerid | An index according to the date and time of the recording, intersected with the caller ID of the recording. |

> I'm not a DBA; actually, I'm quite far from it. I'm confident that the above is more or less an overkill, although this is what I've used in my implementation, and it has worked well.

Once all our constraints had been met, we can start thinking about what our application would look like, both from the Asterisk dialplan side and from the user interface side.

## Step 3: Detailed call flow charts

As with any other application, we are required to create a flow chart describing our application. In our case, the flow chart will describe what happens in the recorder, as a call traverses it. Let's examine the following flow chart:

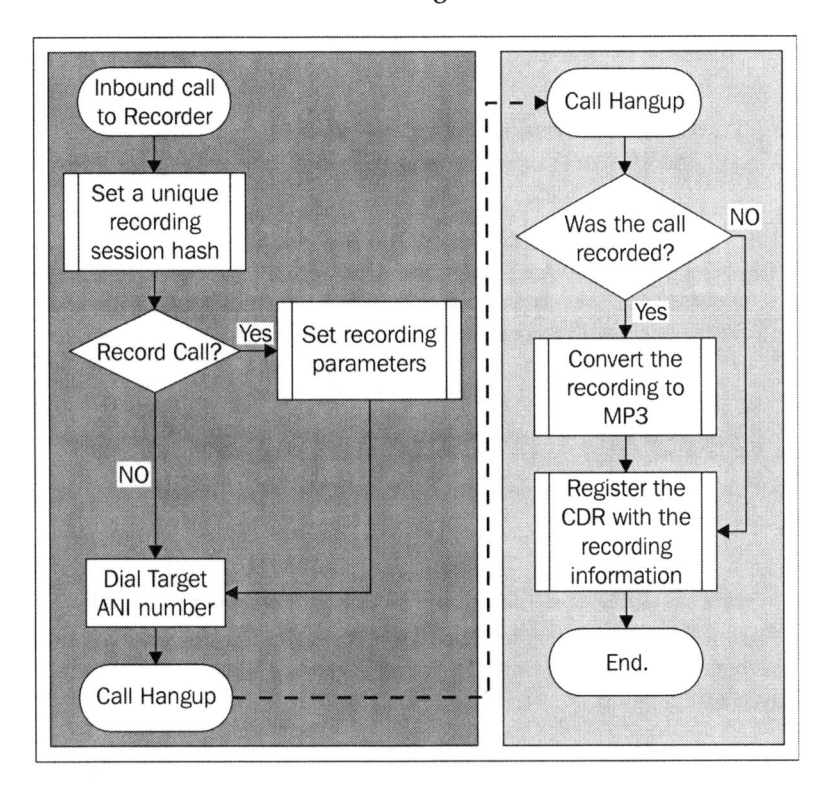

The flow chart illustrates a two stage recording operation—one that is conducted prior to the actual call and the other that is performed after the call has terminated. Let's examine the left-hand side of the flowchart.

As you can see, we are required to assign a unique session hash identified to our call (later on used as the `uniqueid` in the database). We then check if we are required to record the call (according to a preset rule set, defined with the caller's ID). Once we've established whether the call should be recorded or not, we set the recording parameters and then perform the actual dial. Once the call is completed, our execution flow is handed to the right-hand of the diagram.

As a call is terminated, we need to check if the call was recorded or not. If it was recorded, we need to convert the recording to an MP3 file, to be stored in the archive. If the call was not recorded, we simply register the CDR and finish.

## Step 4: The Asterisk dialplan context

It is clear that our context will have two main extensions defined in it—a catch-all extension that would simply catch every dial that passes through the context, and the h extension to be invoked upon the finalization of a call.

Generally speaking, our dialplan will look similar to the following:

```
[recorder]
exten => _X.,1,[Do the recording flow chart]
exten => h,1,[Do the call registration and compression flow chart]
```

> Ok, I admit this is far too general. But my aim here is to have you start thinking about how the implementation actually works. As I indicated at the beginning, this is a programming project/challenge. So it's your task to figure out what the dialplan really looks like.

## Step 5: Develop your human interfaces

No system is complete without a proper human interface. In our case, the interface will be a web-based interface.

> **Alert**: This is not a web developer's book, but an Asterisk book!
>
> True, this is an Asterisk book, so I won't go about and start explaining the basics of web development. However, here are a few pointers to help you get started faster.

When developing a web interface, it is very important that you standardize your development. This means that you need to go about and conform to some form of web development toolkit of framework. As this book uses PHP, I suggest that you try Zend Framework, Code-Igniter, or Kohana, all of which are valid options. Each one of these will make sure that you don't go about and create a mess of display and logic together, making for a really clean web interface implementation. Here are some URLs to get you started with your web interface:

- CodeIgniter—http://www.codeigniter.com
- KohanaPHP—http://www.kohanaphp.org
- Zend Framework—http://framework.zend.com
- CakePHP—http://www.cakephp.org

If you want to make your interface spiffy and shiny, you most probably will look into some JavaScript/AJAX frameworks. Here is a short list of the ones I've been using for a while now:

- DOJO—http://www.dojotoolkit.org
- jQuery—http://www.jquery.com
- Scriptaculous—http://script.aculo.us/

## Step 6: Test, test, and test again

As with any other computer application, make sure that you test your system. A recording system requires not only functionality testing, but also performance testing, to verify whether it can handle the load.

Devise a set of tests to examine the system, test each scenario, and evaluate your results.

Your target number is: being able to record up to 120 concurrent calls.

> The above steps illustrate what I do whenever I'm confronted with a new Asterisk application project (well, not exactly like that, but you get the idea). As you gain experience, you would notice that you are able to skip portions of the process. However, the general manner will always remain.

# Additional programming projects

The following is a list of additional projects that you may find interesting, each one with its own unique set of challenges and constraints. I'm confident that these may inspire you with ideas about possible uses for Asterisk.

## Click-2-Call

Click-2-Call applications have become the latest craze in the telephony business over the past few years. Companies such as Jajah, Mobivox, and others have created various click-2-call applications, lowering the rate of international calling around the world.

> **Personal Disclosure:** The first application I ever wrote for Asterisk was a click-2-call application, way back in 2003. To this day, I'm still developing various click-2-call applications for various companies, each one with a different twist.

# Jajah.Com

Jajah made its name by providing low cost, highly reliable, highly available international web-based callback services. Essentially speaking, web-based callback services are a derivative of click-2-call applications. Click-2-call applications include (but are not limited to) the following: web-based callback, predictive dialers, preview dialers, and others.

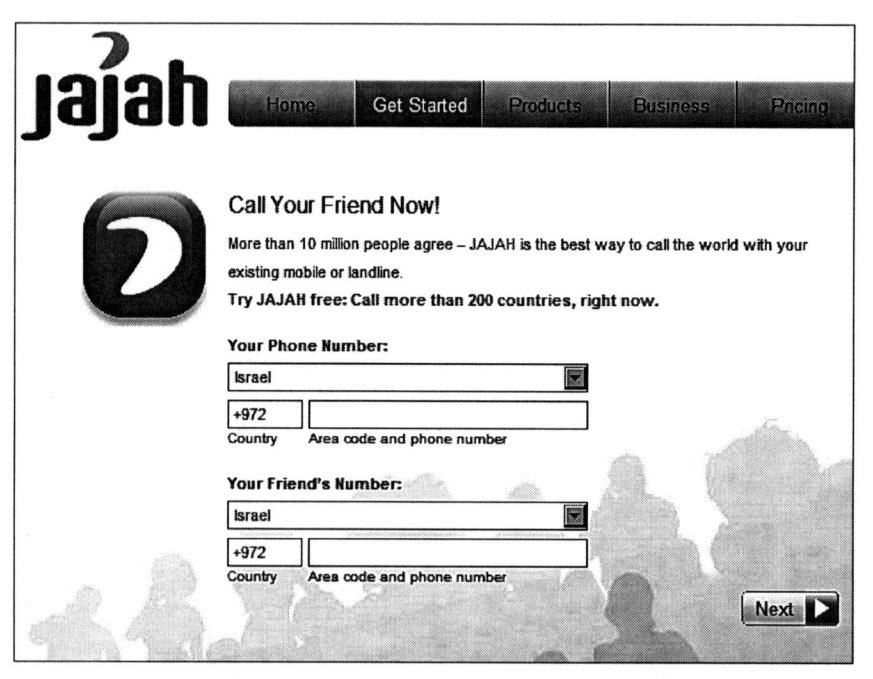

# Stateful call masking

**Stateful call masking** is a call masking service, capable of assigning a single (or more) local **DID** (**Direct Inward Dial**) number (or numbers) to multiple target ANI numbers, while preserving the call routing mask according to the caller ID.

Too complicated? I'll simplify. Let's examine the following diagram:

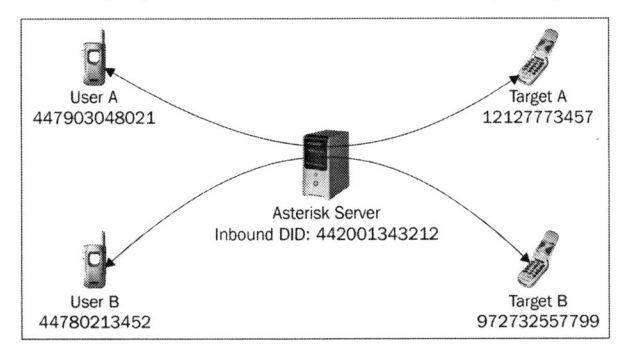

The left-hand of the diagram illustrates the location where the system is active (in our case the UK), while the right-hand side illustrates various call targets. A stateful call masking service will be able to assign the inbound DID number (**442001343212**) to any of the ANI numbers on the right-hand side, according to the inbound caller ID.

One of the services that started out as a stateful call masking service is Rebtel. Actually, what Rebtel did was a little more complicated, as they also modified the outbound caller ID number on the receiving end, allowing the receiver to call back the initiator, without changing the number.

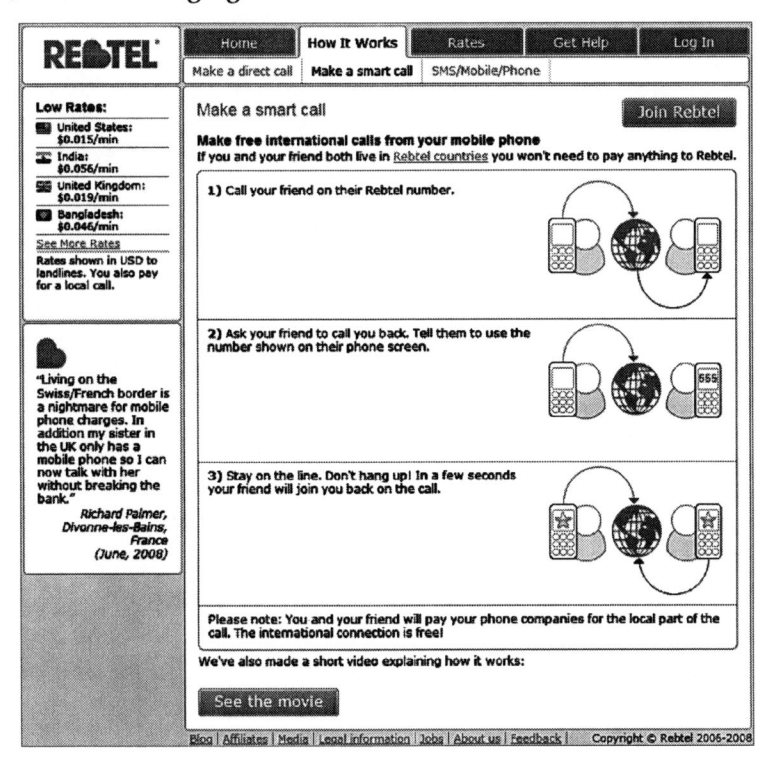

## Punk'ed call

Punk'ed calls are a combination of a preview dialer (click-2-call subset) and a set of recordings and/or a text-to-speech engines. Punk'ed calls are the next step in the evolution of the everlasting "prank call". With Punk'ed call, you can play a prank on the entire city at the same time. Well, this is not something that I would recommend doing, but it's funny and can be done with Asterisk—so why not?

## Date rescue call

You are most probably familiar with this scenario: you've been set up on a blind date with a friend of a friend's girlfriend. You are sitting in the coffee shop, or wherever you had agreed to meet, slowly nibbling on your nails, hoping that your blind date doesn't turn up to be the most horrific creature on the face of the planet. At this point you wish to yourself: "I wish I could have had a friend call me up in the middle of the date. If the date goes bad, I'll excuse myself with the reason that I need to go and help him out. If the date goes nice, I'll notify him that everything is going fine."

Date rescue call is exactly that kind of a friend. You only have to pretend that you are actually talking to someone on the phone. You will need to set up your Asterisk server to call you at a specific date and time, and start playing back some pre-recorded message.

> **Personal Disclosure:** I've actually used my Asterisk servers as a "Date rescue call" system when I was on the dating circuit. Today I'm happily married. While this may sound targeted at a male audience, it is equally applicable to our feminine readers.

## Conference bridge

Conference bridges are one of the cornerstones of modern business practices. I can't even imagine doing business with people without having the ability to conduct a multiple participant conference call.

The main problems with conference calls are usually these:

- Conference services are usually limited to a geographic area, typically a specific country.
- Conference services are usually limited by the number of concurrent participants.
- Generating a recording from a conference call isn't simple, and providers usually charge an arm and a leg for that.

- Even if I do get a recording of a conference call, that recording is highly volatile, meaning that it is usually not digitally signed. If the recording has been modified or tampered with, there is no direct way of knowing this.

Asterisk includes a conference application called MeetMe. Using MeetMe and a smart provisioning database, you can create your own conference bridge that can easily overcome these limitations. In addition, using services such as DIDX and DIDWW will enable you to assign globally available access numbers to your service, thus making your service available worldwide.

# Summary

By now, your mind should be racing with ideas for various projects and applications, applicable to the telephony world and especially to Asterisk. The projects listed previously have been created in the past and are available in various forms. Websites such as www.freeconference.com, www.didww.com and www.didx.net couldn't have existed without the existence of Asterisk, as it has lowered the bar on the entry level for the creation of such services.

Let your imagination run wild, and see where it takes you.

# 10
# Scaling Asterisk Applications

*The more sophisticated we get, the more advanced our buildings and vehicles become, the more vulnerable we are.* - Stephen Ambrose

While Stephen Ambrose's quote relates mainly to general engineering, the same concept applies to software development in general, and Asterisk AGI/AMI programming in particular. Unlike most programming languages or frameworks, Asterisk is constantly in a state of development and flux. It thus makes the entire Asterisk framework evolve at a rapid pace, enabling new features, new API structures, new paradigms, and more stability.

A while back, I was part of a panel discussing the validity of scripting languages as programming languages. As you may know, scripting languages such as PERL, PHP, Ruby, and python are very easy to learn, do not require any special development environment, and will let you get up and running really fast. Programming languages such as C, C++, C#, and Java, usually require the utilization of a compiler and linker, making the development process slightly more complex and also making it slower. Part of the debate during the panel was: "Can scripting languages be considered as programming languages?" While the actual debate isn't important at this point, one of the issues that arose from the debate was: "Languages like PHP and Ruby allow an inexperienced developer to create ingenious applications, without the need to actually learn any specific development paradigm. However, while it makes things easy, it allows the unskilled developer a huge margin of error, thereby creating a highly unmaintainable code". To be honest, I couldn't argue with that issue, as we have more and more PHP/Ruby projects out there, created by non-developers, usually consisting of multiple lines of code without any distinct structure.

Asterisk, as a framework, provides similar flexibility to the developer, allowing a non-experienced developer to create an **IVR/CTI (Interactive Voice Response/ Computer Telephony Integration)** application at ease. As the number of Asterisk built-in functions and applications grows, the number of people using it will grow, and the entry bar for developing applications will come down dramatically. This chapter will try to deal with some of the more advanced topics of developing Asterisk applications—mainly, scalability and performance issues.

# Scaling Asterisk platforms

Most developers, who begin to work with Asterisk, end up developing platforms that look more or less like the following diagram:

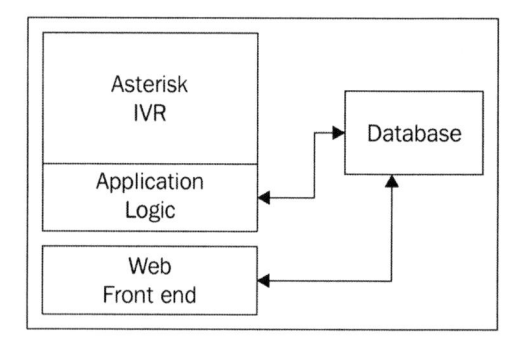

```
┌─────────────┐
│  Asterisk   │
│    IVR      │         ┌──────────┐
├─────────────┤ ──────▶ │ Database │
│ Application │ ◀────── │          │
│    Logic    │         └──────────┘
├─────────────┤             ▲
│    Web      │ ────────────┘
│  Front end  │
└─────────────┘
```

Well, as long as your application is more or less static in size, the above design may surely allow you to run your application smoothly and easily. However, like any other service-oriented platform, any Asterisk platform tends to grow over the course of time.

> Believe or not, IVR services are serious money makers around the world. IVR-based dating services and conferencing services can easily generate thousands of US dollars per month (for the service operator), thereby making it essential to enable rapid and stable scaling of the platform.

So, in order to scale the system, you would most probably say: "No problem, everything is handled by the database, so let's just put in more Asterisk servers and we're done!" However, you must bear in mind that your database server also has limitations, and that the web front end imposes an unknown stress factor on the platform. It is also possible that while a web user is generating a large report, the entire platform performance is degraded for that period of time; our intention is to negate that option.

We shall introduce several technologies and paradigms of platform development that will assist you in scaling up your Asterisk platforms at a greater ease than before.

# Database query caching

One of the most problematic issues with scaling any application is the ever annoying database bottleneck. While Asterisk is fully capable of handling hundreds of concurrent calls, and your web front end is fully capable of serving a similar number, combine the two into a single mix, and you would end up with a database that is fairly loaded.

Modern SQL engines such as MySQL and PostgreSQL provide a certain level of caching. However, their caching is fairly limited to certain types of queries being run on the database, and even then, their optimization is questionable at best. Taking that into consideration, it is clear that we require a different approach to query caching—one that is agnostic to the actual database engine, and which is scalable. So, let's turn our attention to memcached.

According to the memcached website (http://www.danga.com/memcached/):

> *memcached is a high-performance, distributed memory object caching system, generic in nature, but intended for use in speeding up dynamic web applications by alleviating database load.*

Ok, that doesn't really say much, does it? In general, memcached will allow you to free up valuable database time and resources, by caching some of the information provided by the database server to the application in an external storage facility.

Let's take a look at how to work with memcached.

# Starting up

Unlike many other UNIX/Linux services, memcached doesn't have a configuration file. It actually uses a set of command line options to run your memcached service. Let's consider the following example:

```
# ./memcached -d -m 2048 -l 192.168.2.52 -p 6636
```

> Technically speaking, memcached doesn't require special privileges. However, binding it to an unprivileged user or a regular user will be a good security practice to follow.

In the above example, memcached is initiated with 2GB of cache memory, with a listening port of TCP 6636 at IP number 192.168.2.52—straightforward, isn't it?

> If you are using a system that is equipped with a lot of memory (more than 8GB of RAM), but, if you are running it in a 32Bit environment, you may initiate multiple memcached daemons to use multiple cache engines. The upper limit of how many engines you can run is in direct relation to the amount of RAM you have. In any case, experiment with your environment to see how much mileage you'll get from it.

## Using it in a script

One of the nice things about memcached is that it has a multitude of programming APIs and libraries. Memcache handling by PHP is now an official part of the PECL project. If you are using a well-known distribution of Linux, there is a high probability that your distribution may already have a pre-packaged memcache. (I would suggest you to refer your distribution documentation for this information.)

As we've seen before, memcached is a TCP socket server. This indicates that memcached is actually a memory-based storage area, where we can store information for later processing or retrieval. So, in other words, our script will need to decide what to cache and when, and then, find out if the information is located in the cache or not.

The decision of what information to cache is entirely your own. Simply bear in mind that the cache should be used for result sets that contain small pieces of information. However, these can take a long time to calculate.

Here's a small example of how to use memcache and PHP (taken from the `http://dev.mysql.com` website):

```php
<?php

$memc = new Memcache;
$memc->addServer('localhost','11211');
?>

<html xmlns="http://www.w3.org/1999/xhtml" xml:lang="en" lang="en">
<head>
  <meta http-equiv="Content-Type" content="text/html; charset=utf-8" />
  <title>Simple Memcache Lookup</title>
</head>
<body>
<form method="post">
  <p><b>Film</b>: <input type="text" size="20" name="film"></p>
<input type="submit">
</form>
<hr/>
```

```php
<?php
   echo "Loading data...\n";
$value = $memc->get($_REQUEST['film']);
if ($value)
  {
    printf("<p>Film data for %s loaded from
           memcache</p>",$value['title']);
    foreach (array_keys($value) as $key)
       {
    printf("<p><b>%s</b>: %s</p>",$key, $value[$key]);
       }
  }
  else
    {
      $con = new mysqli('localhost','sakila','password','sakila') or
        die ("<h1>Database problem</h1>" . mysqli_connect_error());
      $result = $con->query(sprintf('select * from film where title
                     ="%s"',$_REQUEST['film']));
      $row = $result->fetch_array(MYSQLI_ASSOC);
      $memc->set($row['title'],$row);
      printf("<p>Loaded %s from MySQL</p>",$row['title']);
    }
?>
```

In the example that we just saw, we have created a simple form to look up a movie's details, based on the movie's name. As the form is submitted, the first thing that happens is that the script will use the memcache `get` method to check if the movie name appears in the cache. If it doesn't, it will query the MySQL database and store the information in the cache. If the information is already available in the cache, it will output the retrieved result directly from the cache storage.

You are probably wondering what I'm using memcache for; well, the answer to that is—for storing operational values and enumerators. Most of my applications make use of a large number of enumerators. These enumerators are usually stored in a database for easy operations. However, if I was to read my database for every enumerator that I need, I would more or less kill the database. Whenever I initiate my memcached service, it will immediately follow with a memcache population script, populating it with my various enums. As enums may change in the database, I make sure to update the memcache storage once in a while. In addition, I usually initiate two instances of memcache—one for storing various enums and the other for storing actual application related cache. Separating the cache is not really required; I do it for sake of simplicity and consistency.

# Utilization of web services

Web services? Isn't this supposed to be an Asterisk book? Well, it is an Asterisk book, but there is no rule that says: "We shall not use web services with Asterisk!". Ok, putting the funny bits aside, the utilization of web based services for creating highly complex and versatile Asterisk-based services is a key factor in scalability considerations.

Let's consider the previous n-Tier design, where all my Asterisk and web servers are connected directly to the database. It is clear that at some point in time, the database will become overloaded. Ok, so we have memcache for caching some of the information, which is more or less like wrapping a band-aid in order to stop a gusher.

Using memcache-enabled web services, and having your Asterisk and web applications communicate with these web services via a well-known API, will do wonders to your application. If you are familiar with web services, acronyms such as SOAP, WSDL, XML-RPC and REST shouldn't sound strange to you (you may skip to the next section). If you are unfamiliar with web services, we shall introduce you to XML-RPC—one of the simplest, yet highly powerful, web services framework.

## Introduction to XML-RPC

XML-RPC is a specification and set of implementations that allow software running on disparate operating systems and in different environments, to make procedural calls over the Internet (or any other IP-based network).

XML-RPC's remote procedure uses **HTTP POST** as the transport and **XML** as the encoding method. In general, if we were to examine how XML-RPC works, it would look similar to this:

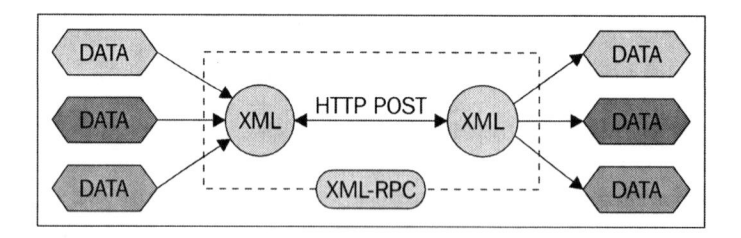

[ The above image is based upon an image from the `http://www.xmlrpc.org` website. ]

Taking the above into consideration, it immediately opens a brand new set of possibilities for companies dealing with Asterisk-based services. Suddenly, you can decouple the application logic from your Asterisk server, thus allowing your developers to focus mainly on developing your business logic, while allowing you to simplify your actual Asterisk application.

Another interesting advantage of using web services for developing Asterisk platform is the ability to outsource portions of the work to someone else—sometimes, in a completely different country. As long as they maintain the XML-RPC API in accordance with your requirements, the platform should work just fine.

## Structure of an XML-RPC request and response

An XML-RPC request is made of two distinct pieces of information—a method and a set of parameters. Parameters may include scalars, numbers, strings, arrays, and so on. Instead of beating about the bush, let's take a look at an XML-RPC request:

```
POST /RPC2 HTTP/1.0
User-Agent: Frontier/5.1.2 (WinNT)
Host: betty.userland.com
Content-Type: text/xml
Content-length: 181

<?xml version="1.0"?>
<methodCall>
   <methodName>examples.getStateName</methodName>
   <params>
      <param>
         <value><i4>41</i4></value>
         </param>
      </params>
</methodCall>
```

The above example initiates a method called `examples.getStateName`, with a value of 41 in the parameters section. Ok, that seems simple enough; so let's take a look at the response:

```
HTTP/1.1 200 OK
Connection: close
Content-Length: 158
Content-Type: text/xml
Date: Fri, 17 Jul 1998 19:55:08 GMT
Server: UserLand Frontier/5.1.2-WinNT

<?xml version="1.0"?>
<methodResponse>
```

```
            <params>
               <param>
                  <value><string>South Dakota</string></value>
               </param>
            </params>
         </methodResponse>
```

Believe it or not, the response is actually formatted in the same manner as the request. Ok, that makes life really simple.

In the previous example we passed a single variable to our remote method. How do we pass more values then? More importantly, how do we distinguish between these values? Here, the `struct` parameter comes to the rescue. It is possible to pass a complete structure as the parameter, thereby allowing the remote server to process the request accordingly.

Here's a small example:

```
POST /RPC2 HTTP/1.0
User-Agent: Frontier/5.1.2 (WinNT)
Host: betty.userland.com
Content-Type: text/xml
Content-length: 181

<?xml version="1.0"?>
<methodCall>
   <methodName>examples.average</methodName>
   <params>
   <struct>
      <member>
         <name>lowerBound</name>
         <value><i4>18</i4></value>
      </member>
      <member>
         <name>upperBound</name>
         <value><i4>139</i4></value>
      </member>
   </struct>
   </params>
</methodCall>
```

Now, imagine that you are writing a prepaid calling card platform. You would like your billing and provisioning system to be based on a Windows system, while Asterisk performs all the voice functionality—you can, definitely. By creating a web service on the Windows provisioning side that is capable of implementing the various functions required for the prepaid platform (such as authenticate user, get credit, validate destination, and so on), you can easily create a highly extendible prepaid calling card platform.

# Apache versus Lighttpd

Apache is the mother of all HTTP servers. Mandriva Linux used to have an **Apache mod_kitchensink module**, where you could browse to your Apache HTTP server with the URL `http://localhost/kitchensink`, only to encounter the following page:

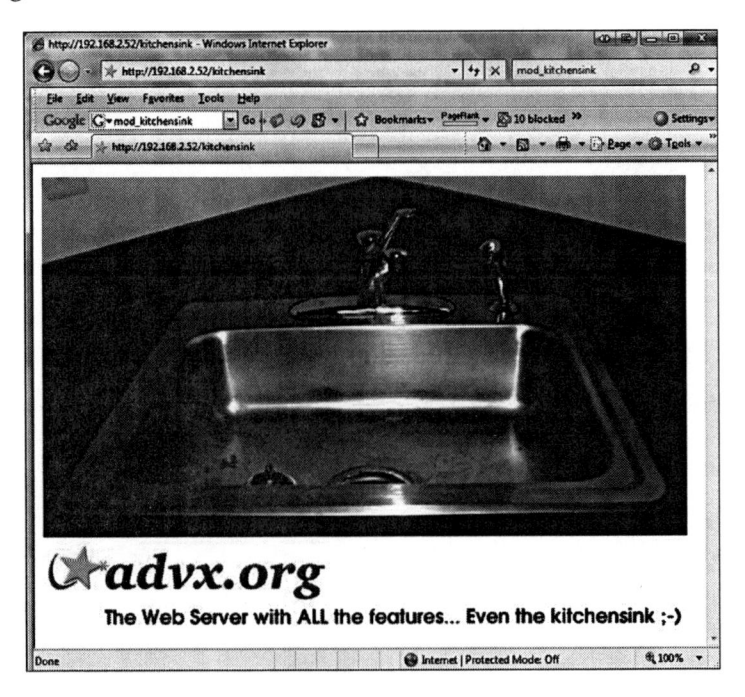

Now, if you get everything in it, including the kitchen sink, how much of it is there that you don't need? Moreover, if Apache is so big, is it really that optimal for your usage?

The answer isn't really all that clear, but one thing is sure: when dealing with a high performance Asterisk system, relying on Apache isn't much of a good idea. You are probably wondering why? Well, in general, the reason would be Apache's ever increasing resource utilization and your web application usage.

Let's take, for example, a highly popular prepaid calling card application such as A2Billing. A2Billing makes use of a highly sophisticated web interface to control each and every aspect of A2Billing. When installing A2Billing for the first time, you are immediately required to increase the amount of memory your PHP environment is allowed to consume. If you don't, your web interface is rendered unusable. As your system grows, these memory requirements tend to grow, especially when generating reports. This is mainly caused by a lack of optimization on behalf of A2Billing. But we are not here to discuss A2Billing's faults.

> The A2Billing website can be found at http://www.a2billing.org

So, let's imagine that I need a maximum PHP environment of 256MB in order for PHP to be able to generate a report with A2Billing. Now imagine that I would have a server with 2 GB RAM, and three people are trying to generate reports at the same time. Oops, the Apache server will simply fail on that one—I should know; I tried it!

In comes Lighttpd to our rescue. Lighttpd is a lightweight, extremely fast HTTP server and reverse proxy. It is equipped with FastCGI modules and PHP modules, enabling it to run PHP-based web pages natively. The added value of Lighttpd is its ability to control the number of instances of a PHP FastCGI server, thereby putting a physical cap on the amount of resources your web interface will consume.

The following configuration is used on one of my production servers, using Lighttpd to serve the A2Billing web interface (no changes were made to the A2Billing web interface):

```
############ Options you really have to take care of
####################

## modules to load
server.modules              = (
                                "mod_rewrite",
                                "mod_redirect",
                                "mod_alias",
                                "mod_access",
                                "mod_auth",
                                "mod_fastcgi",
                                "mod_userdir",
                                "mod_cgi",
                                "mod_accesslog" )

## a static document-root, for virtual-hosting take look at the
## server.virtual-* options
server.document-root        = "/srv/www/lighttpd/"

## where to send error-messages to
server.errorlog             = "/var/log/lighttpd/error.log"

# files to check for if .../ is requested
index-file.names            = ( "index.php", "index.html",
                                "index.htm", "default.htm" )

## set the event-handler (read the performance section in the manual)
```

```
# server.event-handler = "freebsd-kqueue" # needed on OS X
# mimetype mapping
mimetype.assign             = (
  ".rpm"          =>      "application/x-rpm",
  ".pdf"          =>      "application/pdf",
  ".sig"          =>      "application/pgp-signature",
  ".spl"          =>      "application/futuresplash",
  ".class"        =>      "application/octet-stream",
  ".ps"           =>      "application/postscript",
  ".torrent"      =>      "application/x-bittorrent",
  ".dvi"          =>      "application/x-dvi",
  ".gz"           =>      "application/x-gzip",
  ".pac"          =>      "application/x-ns-proxy-autoconfig",
  ".swf"          =>      "application/x-shockwave-flash",
  ".tar.gz"       =>      "application/x-tgz",
  ".tgz"          =>      "application/x-tgz",
  ".tar"          =>      "application/x-tar",
  ".zip"          =>      "application/zip",
  ".mp3"          =>      "audio/mpeg",
  ".m3u"          =>      "audio/x-mpegurl",
  ".wma"          =>      "audio/x-ms-wma",
  ".wax"          =>      "audio/x-ms-wax",
  ".ogg"          =>      "application/ogg",
  ".wav"          =>      "audio/x-wav",
  ".gif"          =>      "image/gif",
  ".jar"          =>      "application/x-java-archive",
  ".jpg"          =>      "image/jpeg",
  ".jpeg"         =>      "image/jpeg",
  ".png"          =>      "image/png",
  ".xbm"          =>      "image/x-xbitmap",
  ".xpm"          =>      "image/x-xpixmap",
  ".xwd"          =>      "image/x-xwindowdump",
  ".css"          =>      "text/css",
  ".html"         =>      "text/html",
  ".htm"          =>      "text/html",
  ".js"           =>      "text/javascript",
  ".asc"          =>      "text/plain",
  ".c"            =>      "text/plain",
  ".cpp"          =>      "text/plain",
  ".log"          =>      "text/plain",
  ".conf"         =>      "text/plain",
  ".text"         =>      "text/plain",
  ".txt"          =>      "text/plain",
```

```
                ".dtd"          =>      "text/xml",
                ".xml"          =>      "text/xml",
                ".mpeg"         =>      "video/mpeg",
                ".mpg"          =>      "video/mpeg",
                ".mov"          =>      "video/quicktime",
                ".qt"           =>      "video/quicktime",
                ".avi"          =>      "video/x-msvideo",
                ".asf"          =>      "video/x-ms-asf",
                ".asx"          =>      "video/x-ms-asf",
                ".wmv"          =>      "video/x-ms-wmv",
                ".bz2"          =>      "application/x-bzip",
                ".tbz"          =>      "application/x-bzip-compressed-tar",
                ".tar.bz2"      =>      "application/x-bzip-compressed-tar",
                # default mime type
                ""              =>      "application/octet-stream",
         )
         #### accesslog module
         accesslog.filename          = "/var/log/lighttpd/access.log"

         ## deny access the file-extensions
         #
         # ~    is for backupfiles from vi, emacs, joe, ...
         # .inc is often used for code includes which should in general not be
              part
         #     of the document-root
         url.access-deny             = ( "~", ".inc" )
         $HTTP["url"] =~ "\.pdf$" {
           server.range-requests = "disable"
         }
         ##
         # which extensions should not be handle via static-file transfer
         #
         # .php, .pl, .fcgi are most often handled by mod_fastcgi or mod_cgi

              static-file.exclude-extensions = ( ".php", ".pl", ".fcgi" )

         ######### Options that are good to be but not neccesary to be changed
         #######
         ## bind to port (default: 80)
         server.port                 = 80

         ## bind to localhost (default: all interfaces)
         #server.bind                = "127.0.0.1"

         ## to help the rc.scripts
         server.pid-file             = "/var/run/lighttpd.pid"

         ## change uid to <uid> (default: don't care)
         server.username             = "apache"
```

```
## change uid to <uid> (default: don't care)
server.groupname        = "apache"

#### fastcgi module
fastcgi.server          = ( ".php" =>
                            ( "localhost" =>
                              (
                                "socket" => "/var/run/lighttpd/php-
fastcgi.socket",
                                "bin-path" => "/usr/bin/php-cgi",
                                "max-procs" => 1,
                                "min-procs" => 1
                              )
                            )
                          )

#### CGI module
cgi.assign              = ( ".pl"  => "/usr/bin/perl",
                            ".cgi" => "/usr/bin/perl" )
```

For more information about the Lighttpd web server, please refer to the project website, located at http://www.lighttpd.net/.

## Virtualization and cloud computing

The latest craze in the IT industry is virtualization and cloud computing. Virtualization solutions are popping up all over the IT spectrum, ranging from the well established VMWARE (now an EMC company), via XEN (now a Citrix-backed project), to OpenVZ (an Open Source KVM). Virtualization surely is the hottest thing around. Cloud computing isn't all that common yet. However, solutions such as Amazon's EC2 platform are available from various cloud computing providers, making virtualization technologies available to everybody, at a fraction of the cost.

One of the aspects of building highly scalable platforms is their ability to scale well within a virtualization environment or a cloud computing environment. However, these pose some interesting issues, directly related to both Asterisk and the virtualization technology being used.

Before we continue further, we must first understand a few concepts of virtualization technologies—mainly the difference between the mainstream virtualization techniques.

> This is not a book about virtualization, so we won't go into this subject in depth. However, we will try to evaluate the various aspects of using Asterisk within a virtualization framework.

## Full virtualization

**Full virtualization** refers to the ability to implement a full hardware simulation of the underlying computer hardware, in software. While the concept has been known since the late 1960s, the first commercially-viable product for full virtualization on the PC was VMWARE, back in 1998. The added value of full virtualization is that it will support any operating system, without any requirement for special hardware.

## Hardware-assisted virtualization

The idea behind **Hardware-assisted virtualization** is that the underlying hardware provides some facilities of virtualization—mainly related to the CPU running the guest operating system. The idea is that the guest operating system and the host operating system share a common instruction set, thereby allowing for accelerated performance by offloading some of the work back to the CPU from the host operating system's virtual CPU. XEN refers to this ability as **Hardware Virtual Machine (HVM)**.

## Paravirtualization

In **Paravirtualization**, the guest operating system offers each of the host operating systems, a software interface, which is similar to the underlying hardware—not identical though. This immediately results in the requirement to port each of the host operating systems to support the guest operating system's **Virtual Machine Monitor (VMM)**. The main issue with paravirtualization is that it would be able to execute most open source operating systems. However, when dealing with operating systems such as Windows that can't be fully ported—well, I'll let you complete the sentence.

> There are a few others, but these are the main ones that you will encounter along the way.

## Asterisk in a virtualized environment

First things first. If you are working within a virtualized environment and hope to work with any hardware interface card, you can be sure to run into issues. In this situation, the only virtualization solution you can use would be the one that uses Hardware-assisted virtualization or Kernel virtualization (not explained here). But again, the task isn't that simple.

Now, let's imagine for the sake of argument that you don't require any PSTN interfacing, and that you rely completely on VoIP. Life is much simpler at this point. So, in theory, going to a virtualization solution should be easy—Wrong!

Asterisk is a CPU and I/O hog—an I/O hog to be more accurate. That is because each SIP call requires UDP sockets. These are more or less file descriptors from the OS level, thus, it's I /O. File writing and playback also requires I/O. So, in general, almost any operation that Asterisk performs, relies heavily on I/O functionality.

What is the best virtualization environment for Asterisk? That is dependent on your I/O consumption. Isn't the I/O consumption of Asterisk a well-known figure? The answer is no, as it is dependent on how you use Asterisk. For example, an Asterisk server not dealing with transcoding of media and handling SIP traffic that is fully capable of being re-invited, will consume much less I/O than an Asterisk server that is required to do Media pass through.

Confusing? Indeed it is! Here is something from my personal experience. Some of the projects I've done involved the usage of both VMWARE Server and VMWARE Server ESX. While some projects that dealt mainly with a calling card application were capable of handling up to 90 concurrent channels of Media pass through audio, another platform that was dealing mainly with re-invites was fully capable of handling up to 300 channels per virtual server.

If you are thinking of using either virtualization or cloud computing, it is imperative that you perform full regression testing of your application and your installation. While virtualization and cloud computing allow for fairly rapid growth, the added value of rapid growth is immediately negated by an improper choice of virtualization technology.

# Summary

Congratulations! You have reached the final chapter of this book and you are now well-equipped with the information required to build the next Verizon Killer application. Regardless of whether you are the next Vonage, JaJah, or simply the neighborhood call shop, I hope this book has assisted you in your quest for Asterisk development knowledge and know-how.

If you would like to get in touch with me, you are welcome to visit my blog at `http://www.simionovich.com`, where I share my insights and thoughts about Asterisk, technology, open source, and life in general.

# Index

## A

**A2Billing** 185, 186
**A2Billing™**
  about 120
  web site, for project 121
**AA.** *See* **automatic attendant**
**ACRG**
  features 162
  PSTN 163
  requirements 162
**actions, AMI 146**
**ADSI programming application 24**
**AGI**
  about 75
  AGI script, execution flow 81, 82
  and Asterisk, diagrammatic
    representation 94
  application, information 80
  DeadAGI 77, 78
  dialplan, documentation 80
  Enhanced Asterisk Gateway Interface
    (EAGI) 77
  execution flow 81-83
  FastAGI 78
  methods 83, 84
  programming languages,
    applicability 76, 77
  scripting, frameworks 80
  working 76
**AGI/Dialplan**
  about 106
  agiWrapper.agi script 110, 111
  Atomic-AGI 107
  Atomic-AGI, dial-plan example 108
  SetSessionID.agi script 108

**AGI script.** *See also* **AGI**
  about 92
  A2Billing™ 120
  debugging 100
  developing, rules 84
  FastAGI 123
  FreePBX™ 119
  hello-world.php 98, 99
  hello-world program 95
  invoking 76
  permissions 92
  PHP based 93
  STDIN (Standard Input) data stream 76
  STDOUT (Standard Output) data stream 76
**AGI script, developing rules**
  Asterisk channel, using 85
  balancing, dialplan logic used 87
  balancing, web services used 87
  binary compiles 86, 87
  blocking applications, restricting 85
  internet, using 88, 89
  syslog, using 88
  termination 85
  Virtual Machine (VM) based languages,
    restricting 86
**AJAM 158**
**AJAX Enabled Manager.** *See* **AJAM**
**AMI**
  actions 146
  actions, sending to 147, 150
  and PHPAGI 148
  asynchronous originate actions 155
  basics 146
  event/action, types 145
  event call backs 151
  events 146

history 143
interacting with 150
invoking 148
invoking, PHPAGI class used 149
logging in 147
logging off 148
PHPAGI originate, for versions 1.0 and 1.2 154
PHPAGI originate, for versions 1.4 and 1.6 154
proxy servers 158
with Asterisk 1.0 and 1.2 145
with Asterisk 1.4 and 1.6 146
working 144

**AMP** 7

**Apache**
vs Lighttpd 185-189

**applications, dialplan**
about 41
IVR application, creating 41

**ARI** 165

**Asterisk**
ACRG 162
additional applications 69
addons stable source code, downloading 11
AGI/Dialplan 106
AGI script, debugging 100
AGI script, PHP based 93
AJAM 158
AMI 143
AMI proxy servers 158
and AGI, diagrammatic representation 94
application section GUI 24
Asynchronous JavaScript and XML Asterisk Manager (AJAM) 158
busy application 69
call recording gateway 162
call recording gateway, features 162
channel drivers 25
click-2-call application, creating 155
code, compiling 26
configuring 23
congestion application 69
ControlPlayback application 70
DAHDI and Zaptel, differences 21
dialplan 32
dialplan, syntax 33
Digium Asterisk Hardware Device Interface (DAHDI) 10
Digium hardware 9
downloading 8
Exec application 65
ExecIf application 65
FastAGI 123
Gosub directive 63, 64
GosubIf directive 63
Goto application 59
GotoIf application 60
in virtualized environment 190, 191
Libpri 10
MacroExclusive application 69
macros application 69
MixMonitor application 72
Monitor application 71
MusicOnHold application 73
open source PBX 11
options, defining for compiling 23
originate manager action 155, 156
PHPAGI 103
PHP-CLI vs PHP-CGI 91
php.ini configuration file 92
platforms, scaling 178
project implementation, guidelines 163
SayAlpha application 70
SayDigits application 70
SayNumber application 71
source code, compiling 13
source-stable source code, downloading 11
state machines 32
StopMixMonitor application 72
StopMonitor application 72
SVN source packages 12
TryExec application 66
version 1.6.X, for argument passing to FastAGI 125
versions 1.2.X and 1.4.X, for argument passing to FastAGI 125
versions 1.2.X, for FastAGI error handling 126
versions 1.4.X and 1.6.X, for FastAGI error handling 126
virtual timer kernel module 9
web site, for variables 38
writing expressions 61

Zaptel 9
**Asterisk 1.2.X**
  version, for FastAGI error handling 126
**Asterisk 1.2.X and 1.4.X**
  versions, for argument passing
    to FastAGI 125
**Asterisk 1.4.X and 1.6.X**
  versions, for FastAGI error handling 126
**Asterisk 1.6.X**
  version, for argument passing
    to FastAGI 125
**Asterisk2Billing.** *See* **A2Billing™**
**Asterisk application**
  busy application 69
  congestion application 69
  ControlPlayback application 70
  Exec application 65
  ExecIf application 65
  Gosub directive 63
  GosubIf directive 63
  Goto application 59
  GotoIf application 59
  MacroExclusive application 69
  macros application 67
  MixMonitor application 72
  Monitor application 71
  MusicOnHold application 73
  read application 56
  SayAlpha application 70
  SayDigits application 70
  SayNumber application 71
  StopMixMonitor application 72
  StopMonitor application 72
  TryExec application 66
**Asterisk Call Recording Gateway.** *See*
    **ACRG**; *See* **ACRG**
**Asterisk channel** 58
**Asterisk CLI** 53
**Asterisk JAVA**
  about 141
  drawbacks 141
**Asterisk Gateway Interface.** *See* **AGI**
**Asterisk Management Portal.** *See* **AMP**
**Asterisk platforms, scaling**
  about 178
  database query, caching 179
  web services, utilizing 182

**Asterisk Recording Interface.** *See* **ARI**; *See*
    **ARI**
**Asterisks Manager Interface.** *See* **AMI**
**Asynchronous JavaScript Asterisk Manager.**
    *See* **AJAM**
**Atomic** 107
**Atomic-AGI**
  about 107
  dial plan, example 108
**auto attendant.** *See* **automatic attendant**
**automatic attendant, IVR application**
  about, 42
  application, answer, 44
  application, background, 48, 49
  application, dial, 44-47
  application, EndWhile, 50
  application, Hangup, 49
  application, playback, 48
  application, SoftHangup, 49
  application, WaitExten, 49
  applications, 43
  code, 51
  code, debugging, 53
  code, dialed extensions management, 52
  code, error trapping, 52
  code, main context body, 51
  flow chart, 42, 43

# B

**binary compiled** 77
**built-in channel variables, dialplan**
  ${CALLERID(all)} 37
  ${CALLERID(name)} 38
  ${CALLERID(num)} 38
  ${CHANNEL} 38
  ${CONTEXT} 38

# C

**Call Detail Records** 115
**CDRs** 115
**click-2-call application**
  AMI proxy servers 158
  Asterisk originate manager action 155, 156
  Asynchronous JavaScript Asterisk Manager
    (AJAM) 158, 159
  Jabka 156, 157

cloud computing. *See* **virtualization**
**compiling**
  Asterisk 23
  Asterisk source code 27
  code 26
  DAHDI kernel module 18
  dahdi-tools 21
  dahdi-tools package 20
  Libpri 22
  source code 13
  Zaptel 14
**Concurrent Versions System.** *See* **CVS**
**configuring**
  Asterisk 23
  dahdi-tools 21
  Zaptel 14
**congestion 69**
**CVS 12**

# D

**DAHDI**
  and Zaptel, differences 21
  dahdi kernel module, installing 18, 19
  dahdi-tools, compiling 21
  dahdi-tools, installing 21
  dahdi-tools package, compiling 20
  downloading 10
  kernel module, compiling 18
**database query, caching**
  memcached, starting up 179, 180
  memcached, using in script 180, 181
**DeadAGI 77**
**dialplan**
  applications 41
  context 32, 33
  extension 33, 34
  finite state machines (FSM) 32
  macro, example 67
  macro, executing 68
  syntax 33
  variables 37
**Digium Asterisk Hardware Device Interface.** *See* **DAHDI**
**Digium hardware 9**
**downloading**
  Asterisk 8

Asterisk-addons stable source code, downloading 11
DAHDI 10
Libpri source code 10,11
source-stable source code 11
Zaptel 9
**Dual-tone multi-frequency.** *See* **DTMF;** *See* **DTMF**
**DTMF 56**

# E

**EAGI 77**
**Enhanced Asterisk Gateway Interface.** *See* **EAGI**
**events, AMI 146**
**Exec application 65**
**ExecIf application 65**
**extension, dialplan**
  a extension 36
  context inclusion 34
  failed extension 36
  fax extension 36
  [general] context 35
  [global] context 35
  h extension 36
  i extension 36
  o extension 36
  pattern matching, example 35
  pattern matching, rules 35
  s extension 36
  special extension 36
  t extension 36
  T extension 36
  talk extension 36

# F

**FastAGI**
  about 124
  argument handling 124, 125
  arguments passing, Asterisk 1.2.X and 1.4.X used 79
  arguments passing, Asterisk 1.6.X used 79
  error handling 125
  frameworks 79
  other tool kits 140
  PHPAGI and Google 133

with PHPAGI and Google 133
with PHPAGI and xinetd 126
**FastAGI argument handling**
  Asterisk version 1.2.X and 1.4.X 125
  Asterisk version 1.6.X 125
**FastAGI error handling**
  about 125
  Asterisk version 1.2.X 126
  Asterisk version 1.4.X and 1.6.X 126
**FastAGI, other tool kits**
  Asterisk::FastAGI module 140,141
  Asterisk-JAVA 141
  Perl module 140
**FastAGI, PHPAGI and Google used**
  about 133
  FastAGI.php 139
  fastagiServer.php 139, 140
  httpd.php 134
  httpServer.php 135-138
**FastAGI, PHPAGI and xinetd used**
  about 126
  fastagiWrapper.php bootstrap 130-133
  PHPAPI, configuring 130
  xinetd, about 127
  xinetd, configuring 128, 129
**finite state machine.** *See* **FSM**
**Free Telephone Services**
         **Corporation.** *See* **FTSC**
**FreePBX™**
  about 119,120
  website, for project 120
**FSM.** *See also* **state machines**
**FSM** 32
**FTSC** 114

# G

**Gosub directive** 63-65
**GosubIf directive** 63-65
**Goto application** 59, 60
**GotoIf application** 60

# H

**Hardware Virtual Machine.** *See* **HVM**
**HVM** 190

# I

**inheritance** 40
**installing**
  Asterisk 23
  DAHDI kernel module 18
  dahdi-tools 21
  Libpri 22
  Zaptel 16,17
**Interactive Voice Response.** *See* **IVR**
**interpreted language** 77
**IVR** 7, 31
**IVR application, creating**
  application, answer 44
  application, background 48, 49
  application, dial 44-47
  application, EndWhile 50
  application, hangup 49
  application, playback 48
  application, SoftHangup 49
  application, WaitExten 49
  automatic attendant 42
  automatic attendant, applications 43
  automatic attendant code 50
  automatic attendant, code 51
  automatic attendant code, context body 51
  automatic attendant code, debugging 53
  automatic attendant code, dialed extensions
         management 52
  automatic attendant code, error trapping 52
  automatic attendant code, main context
         body 51
  automatic attendant code, testing 53
**IVR services** 178

# J

**Jabka, click-2-call application** 156, 157, 158

# K

**kernel module, compiling** 18

# L

**Lesser General Public License.** *See* **LGPL**
**LGPL** 104
**Libpri**

compiling 22
installing 22
source code, downloading 10,11
**Lighttpd**
  vs Apache 185-189

# M

**MacroExclusive application 69**
**macros**
  about 67
  example 67
  executing 68
  variable, ${MACRO_CONTEXT} 68
  variable, ${MACRO_EXTEN} 68
  variable, ${MACRO_OFFSET} 68
  variable, ${MACRO_PRIORITY} 68
  variables, about 68
**mathematical manipulation, variables 38,39**
**memcached**
  about 179
  starting up 179, 180
  using, in script 180, 181

# O

**open source PBX system 11**

# P

**PBX system 11**
**PHP**
  based, AGI scripts 93
  PHPAGI, AGI class library 103
  php.ini configuration file 92
**php.ini configuration file 92**
**PHP-CGI**
  vs PHP-CLI 91
**PHP-CLI**
  vs PHP-CGI 91
**PHPAGI**
  about 103
  additional files 104
  class library file,
        phpagi-asmanager.php 104
  class library file, phpagi.php 104
  fastagi.xinetd file 104
  file structure 104

LGPL 104
obtaining 104
phpagi-asmanager.php,
      originate function 153, 154
phpagi.conf.example file 104
phpagi-fastagi.php file 104
simple example 104
**PHPAGI AMI, originate**
  about 152, 153
  asynchronous originate actions 155
  for versions 1.0 and 1.2 154
  for versions 1.4 and 1.6 154
  phpagi-asmanager.php function 153
**PHPAGI and AMI**
  actions, sending to AMI 150
  AMI, interacting with 150
  AMI, invoking 148, 149
  AMI invoking, PHPAGI class used 149
  event call backs, AMI 151
**PHPAGI, complex example**
  db_register_cdr.inc.php script module 119
  db_validate_target.inc.php script
        module 117
  FTSC 114
**PHPAGI, simple example 104**
**programming projects**
  click-2-call application 171
  conference bridge 174
  data rescue call 174
  Jajah.Com 172
  Punk'ed calls 174
  stateful call masking 172
**project**
  additional programming projects 171
  click-2-call application 171
  conference bridge 174
  data rescue call 174
  implementation, guidelines 163, 164
  Jajah.com 172
  Punk'ed call 174
  statefull call masking 172
**project implementation, guidelines**
  Asterisk dialplan context 170
  call flow charts 164, 169
  human interface,
        development 164, 170, 171

operational constraints, understanding 163-168
requirements, analysis 163-165
testing procedure 164, 171

# R

read application 56, 57
regular expressions
  about 62
  operator precedence 63

# S

source code, compiling
  dahdi kernel module, installing 18, 19
  dahdi-tools, compiling 21
  dahdi-tools, configuring 20, 21
  dahdi-tools, installing 21
  dahdi-tools package, compiling 20
  kernel module, compiling 18
  Libpri, compiling 22
  Zaptel, compiling 14, 15, 16
  Zaptel, installing 16, 17
SQL Primer, web site 117
state machines
  elements 32
string manipulation, variables
  about 39
  string concatenation 40
  substrings 39
Subversion. *See* SVN
SVN 12
SVN source package, Asterisk
  compilation dependencies 13
  source code packages, downloading 12, 13

# T

TryExec application 66

# U

user input 55, 56

# V

variables, dialplan
  about 37
  built-in variables 37
  channel variables, types 37
  custom variables 38
  mathematical manipulation 38, 39
  scoping 40, 41
  string manipulation 39
  string manipulation, string concatenation 40
  string manipulation, substrings 39
version
  Asterisk-addons stable release version, 1.4.6 used 12
versions
  Asterisk 1.2.X and 1.4.X, for argument passing to FastAGI 125
  Asterisk 1.2.X, for FastAGI error handling 126
  Asterisk 1.4.X and 1.6.X, for FastAGI error handling 126
  Asterisk 1.6.X for argument passing to FastAGI 125
virtualization
  about 189
  full virtualization 190
  hardware-assisted virtualization 190
  Paravirtualization 190
Virtual Machine Monitor. *See* VMM
VMM 190

# W

Web-Callback. *See* click-2-call application
web services, utilizing
  XML-RPC 182, 183
writing expressions
  about 61
  arithmetic operators 62, 63
  comparison operators 62
  logical operators 61, 63
  operators used 61

## X

**XML-RPC**
  about 182, 183
  request, structure 183, 184
  response, structure 183, 184
**XML-RPC request, structure** 183, 184
**XML-RPC response, structure** 183, 184

## Z

**Zapata Telephony Driver.** *See* **Zaptel**
**Zaptel**
  about 9
  and DAHDI, differences 21
  compiling 14, 16
  configuring 14
  downloading 9
  installing 16, 17
  options, defining for compiling 15

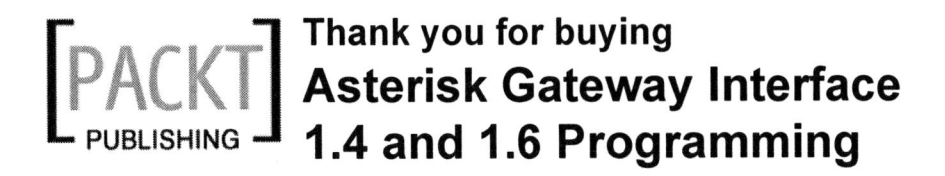

# Thank you for buying
# Asterisk Gateway Interface 1.4 and 1.6 Programming

## Packt Open Source Project Royalties

When we sell a book written on an Open Source project, we pay a royalty directly to that project. Therefore by purchasing Asterisk Gateway Interface Programming, Packt will have given some of the money received to the Asterisk project.

In the long term, we see ourselves and you—customers and readers of our books—as part of the Open Source ecosystem, providing sustainable revenue for the projects we publish on. Our aim at Packt is to establish publishing royalties as an essential part of the service and support a business model that sustains Open Source.

If you're working with an Open Source project that you would like us to publish on, and subsequently pay royalties to, please get in touch with us.

## Writing for Packt

We welcome all inquiries from people who are interested in authoring. Book proposals should be sent to author@packtpub.com. If your book idea is still at an early stage and you would like to discuss it first before writing a formal book proposal, contact us; one of our commissioning editors will get in touch with you.

We're not just looking for published authors; if you have strong technical skills but no writing experience, our experienced editors can help you develop a writing career, or simply get some additional reward for your expertise.

## About Packt Publishing

Packt, pronounced 'packed', published its first book "Mastering phpMyAdmin for Effective MySQL Management" in April 2004 and subsequently continued to specialize in publishing highly focused books on specific technologies and solutions.

Our books and publications share the experiences of your fellow IT professionals in adapting and customizing today's systems, applications, and frameworks. Our solution-based books give you the knowledge and power to customize the software and technologies you're using to get the job done. Packt books are more specific and less general than the IT books you have seen in the past. Our unique business model allows us to bring you more focused information, giving you more of what you need to know, and less of what you don't.

Packt is a modern, yet unique publishing company, which focuses on producing quality, cutting-edge books for communities of developers, administrators, and newbies alike. For more information, please visit our website: www.PacktPub.com.

## Building Telephony Systems With Asterisk

ISBN: 190-4-811-15-9    Paperback: 180 pages

An easy introduction to using and configuring Asterisk to build feature-rich telephony systems for small and medium businesses.

1. Install, configure, deploy, secure, and maintain Asterisk
2. Build a fully-featured telephony system and create a dial plan that suits your needs
3. Learn from example configurations for different requirements

## TrixBox Made Easy

ISBN: 190-4-81-1-930    Paperback: 160 pages

A step-by-step guide to installing and running your home and office VoIP system

1. Plan and configure your own VoIP and telephony systems
2. Setup voicemail, conferencing, and call recording
3. Clear and practical tutorial with case study format

Please check **www.PacktPub.com** for information on our titles

## Building Telephony Systems With Asterisk

ISBN: 978-1-847192-88-2　　　　Paperback: 204 pages

A practical guide for deploying and managing an Asterisk-based telephony system using the AsteriskNOW Beta 6 software appliance

1. Install an Asterisk-based telephony system fast
2. Learn the AsteriskGUI web management interface
2. Configure IP phones and connections
3. Configure and use the conferencing system

## Building Telephony Systems with OpenSER

ISBN: 978-1-847193-73-5　　　　Paperback: 303 pages

A step-by-step guide to building a high performance Telephony System

1. Install, configure, and troubleshoot OpenSER
2. Use OpenSER to build next generation VOIP networks from scratch
3. Learn and understand SIP Protocol and its functionality
3. Integrate MySQL with OpenSER

Please check www.PacktPub.com for information on our titles

Printed in the United Kingdom
by Lightning Source UK Ltd.
136542UK00001B/219/P